Keys to Citizenship

A Guide to Getting Good Support Services for
People with Learning Difficulties

by

Simon Duffy

Published by Paradigm Consultancy &
Development Agency Ltd.

Printed by Colour Jay Ltd.

ISBN: 0-9543068-2-1

Written by Simon Duffy.

Paradigm
8 Brandon Street
Birkenhead
CH41 5HN

Tel: 0870 010 4933
Fax: 0870 010 4934
Email: admin@paradigm-uk.org

www.paradigm-uk.org

This book is meant as a general guide.
We strongly advise you to seek professional legal
or financial advice, before you consider setting
up a Trust or entering into any financial
arrangements. Legislation and guidance
frequently change. Paradigm cannot guarantee
that, by the time you read this, all of the content
of this book will still be current.

CONTENTS

Table of figures

Thanks

I owe so much thanks to so many different people.

- Thanks to all the people who have let me into their lives to help work out how we could organise things better, in particular: Ann, David, Douglas, John Paul, Michael, Trevor, Marie, Tommy R., Tommy M., Patrick, Monica, Stephen and in loving memory of Dennis, Brian, Margaret, Lynn and Pauline.

- Thanks to all the families who have let me into their lives: especially Mary & Samuel, Bill & Mary, Mary, Jimmy & Margaret, Monica and Stephen & Christine.

- Thanks to all my friends in America and Canada: Especially Marilyn, Lisa, Joanne, Corry, Steve, Steven, Tracy, Hayley and Hayden, Danny and Linda, Ellie, Nan, Lynne, John and Judith. And from Australia: Kevin, Mark, Kate, Felicity and Christine.

- Thanks to all my colleagues from my time in Southwark: Steven, Virginia, Mark (again), Gaby, Annette, Sarah and Susan.

- Thank you to all friends at Inclusion Glasgow: Special thanks to Frances, Doreen, Emma, Suzanne, David, Jean, Sam and Pauline.

- Thanks to everyone in Altrum: Special thanks to John D, John W, Rebecca, Jayne, Diana and Helena.

- Thanks to everyone at Paradigm: Special thanks to Peter, Gill, Judith, Nigel, Susan, Kathy, Suzanne, Ellen, Helen, Wendy, Pam and Nicola.

- Thanks to everybody in North Lanarkshire: In particular Morag, Kathy, Alison, Sharon, Myra, Ann, Leslie, Lynne, Claire, Elaine, Pauline and John.

- Thanks to the IBV Board: Steven, Gary, Peter, Susan and Jan and all those who contributed to it, including Rebecca.

- Thanks to everyone on the board of In Control and everyone who has helped us over the last two years - too many of you to name everybody - but I've got to thank Julie, Helen, Julie, Carl, Caroline and Martin - looks like we pulled it off!

- Love and special thanks to my family: Nicola and Jacob.

Simon Duffy

I also want to give special acknowledgement to those people who read the draft of this book and were kind enough to give me additional stories, comments, ideas and criticisms:

Steven Rose	Pauline Greene
Sharon Ann Fergursson	Kay Mills
Julia Fitzpatrick	Ruth Campbell
Kathy Somers	

I hope I have made this book better with your help. If I haven't, it's my fault.

Preface

Keys to Citizenship was first published in 2003. In 2003, people with a learning disability and their families and carers were starting to have more of a say in how local services needed to change. They were able to do this through the learning disability partnership boards in local areas. Learning disability partnership boards had been set up as part of the government's white paper, Valuing People.A small but growing number of people with a learning disability had more of a say about where they lived, what they did and what support they had. This was possible because of such things as direct payments, supporting people money and the independent living fund. Although these good things were happening for a few people, many people with a learning disability were still not able to live a full and interesting life.Keys to Citizenship helped by trying to give people a practical guide on what was needed in order to live a full and interesting life. In other words, it described what people had a right to expect in order to be treated as an equal citizen. In July 2003, these ideas helped a group of us, including people from the Valuing People Support Team, to think about how everyone with a learning disability might become more in control of their lives. The In Control national programme of change was started. This was set up to see if it was possible to give people with a learning disability more control of their lives by changing how people worked and giving individuals an entitlement to an individual budget. Mencap has been supporting this over the last 2 years and working closely with other organisations. We have been working really hard with individuals and their families and carers and six local authorities to develop this new way of working.

The new chapter that Simon has added this year, in 2005, is called Citizenship: six keys together. It really brings the book up to date. The new chapter describes In Control and how this new way of working will give people the opportunity to play a fuller part in the community and have more control to be able to live their lives as equal citizens.Simon has managed to turn an important and sometimes challenging idea into really practical advice and guidance. I hope the ideas in this book will become more widely available to people with a learning disability and their families and carers.Earlier this year the government published the report Improving the Life Chances of Disabled People and the green paper Independence, well-being and choice: our vision for the future of social care for adults in England. The government says they are committed to finding ways for people to have more control of their lives through individual budgets and the government also describes how In Control is one way of doing this.Many people now believe the future for people with a learning disability is about being more in control, being more involved in the community and about becoming equal and valued citizens. Mencap is committed to these ideas and we will be working with our partners to develop these new ways of working. I believe this book will be a valuable tool and practical guide as we work together to build a better future with and for people with a learning disability and their families and carers.

Jo Williams

Chief Executive

Mencap 2005

About the Author

Simon began working with people with learning difficulties after visiting an NHS hospital and being shocked at the treatment received by people who were forced to live there. From 1990 to 1994 he worked for Southwark Consortium helping to develop new service providers and to design individual services for people who wanted to live in their own homes. In 1994 he won a Harkness Fellowship and spent a year in Denver, Colorado studying the progress of inclusive education and services for children and families in the USA.

Simon returned to the UK in 1995. In 1996 he published *Unlocking the Imagination* that described a new way of thinking about the organisation of human services for people with learning difficulties. In the same year he also founded Inclusion Glasgow, an organisation that delivers individualised support services to people with learning difficulties.

At the beginning of 1999 Simon began work as Director of Consultancy for Paradigm. In 2005 Simon was appointed Director In Control, a new national programme to promote self-directed support. In 2001 Simon completed a PhD in moral philosophy. Simon now lives with Nicola and their son Jacob in Sheffield. He is presently working to improve the funding systems of Local Authorities so that more people can control their own services.

SUMMARY OF THE MAIN POINTS

People with learning difficulties are often badly treated by society and by the services that are paid to help them. A big reason that people with learning difficulties are not treated properly is because they are not given the power to exercise their full rights as human beings. Instead they are treated as objects, controlled by others. People should be treated as full citizens, and in order to make this happen people with learning difficulties need six different things:

1 Self-determination

We have self-determination when other people treat us as people who can speak for ourselves. If we have difficulty in speaking for ourselves then we can get help from other people to achieve self-determination.

2 Direction

We have direction when we know what we are doing, when we have a purpose or a plan for our lives. Although we can all get stuck or taken over by other people's ideas, there is a lot that can be done to help us get our own direction in life. Person Centred Planning tells us about how to get direction.

3 Money

We need money to be a citizen. Not just so we can buy what we need to live, but also so that we can control how we live and how others treat us. It is especially important for people to control the money that is used to pay for their own support services, as this will affect every part of life.

4 Home

We all need a home, a place that belongs to us and where we can belong. Much has been learnt about how we can all have a home, and disabled people are increasingly buying their own homes.

5 Support

We all need help, but if you have a significant learning difficulty this means that you will need ongoing and regular help. This does not mean you have to live a life controlled by other people. There are now many examples of people having help that is really helpful, flexible and individual.

6 Community Life

It is also very important that we play a part in our community. This means working, playing, learning or praying with our fellow citizens and making friends along the way.

This book contains lots of practical things to think about if you want to make improvements in any or all of those areas of your life.

INTRODUCTION: DISCOVERING CITIZENSHIP

The aim of this book is to help people create good individual services for people with learning difficulties. In the jargon which people like me (human service professionals) often use, this book is about 'individual service design'. That means putting together the different kinds of things that are needed to help people live their own lives successfully and safely.

It seems obvious to me that this is something that can only be done one individual at a time and that it must be based upon the views, hopes and dreams of the individual. This seems obvious because I know that my own life needs to be thought about in an individual way. I am me; I am not a stereotype. If you want to give *me* advice about how I should live you need to know who I am for real, not just in terms of your stereotype about me. What is more, you need to make sure that you don't deprive me of the chance to make my own decisions.

This all seems obvious if we think about our own lives and the kind of individuality that we take for granted. But people with learning difficulties are still not thought of as individuals. Until recently government, professional bodies and some charitable organisations still found it difficult to get away from treating people with learning difficulties as one great block of people, perhaps only differentiated by the severity or type of their disability. In this way human beings are simplified down to a label or a diagnosis like 'moderate cognitive disability and severe autism'. A label like that sounds informative, but it really disguises the true identity of the person. If you want to know about someone for real then you need to ask questions like: What do you like to do? Where are you from? What family have you got? What football team do you support? What do you like and dislike? Where do you live? Only the answers to these kinds of questions, and many more like them, are the things that really tell you who someone is. It is these kinds of things that we use to determine how we live and therefore, if we need support, how we should be supported.

So this book will not tell you how to support people with learning difficulties. Instead it is offered as a guide to people with learning difficulties, their families and their allies. It is a DIY guide, a guide on how to go about designing your *own* support service. It contains information about many of the different options that I am aware of. But much more than a set of options, this guide hopes to help you think about the questions you need to ask yourself in order to decide what is right for you.

The central idea, the idea that I use to organise all the ideas and information in this book, is that there are six keys to citizenship. Possession of these six keys together enables us each to achieve full citizenship. The six keys I propose are (1) self-determination, the authority to control our own life; (2) direction, a plan or idea of what we want to achieve; (3) money, to live and to control our own life; (4) a home, a place that is our own, a base for our life; (5) support, help to do the things that we need help to achieve; and (6) a community life, an active engagement in the life of the community and the development of our own network of relationships.

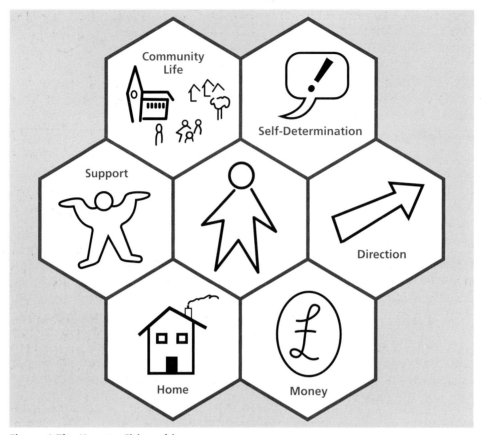

Figure 1 The Keys to Citizenship

Now the idea of 'citizenship' may appear a little unusual; but it is an important idea and I believe it is a very helpful idea for thinking about how best to help people with learning difficulties. Not that citizenship is the point of life; the value of your life does not depend on your being recognised by others as a citizen. Instead citizenship is the word we use to describe what it is to be recognised by other people as an individual who is a full member of the community.

Being seen by others as a citizen is not a guarantee of happiness, fulfilment, long life or personal success. It simply means that other people will take you seriously, treat you as an equal and recognise that you have the dignity of being an individual human being; that you are worthy of respect. Being treated by others in this way does not guarantee happiness; but it does guard against your being abused, it does protect you from being ignored or being treated as simply part of a group.

Citizenship is not the point of life; but being treated as a citizen provides each of us with the best possible foundation for exploring the point of our own individual life. Citizenship protects our individuality and offers us the opportunity to find out, on our own or with others, what we want to do with our lives.

The idea of this book then is to offer six different ways in which we can act to protect or enhance our own citizenship and in particular the citizenship of people with learning difficulties. Of course it could be argued that the community ought to treat everybody as a full citizen anyway; that no one should have to possess self-determination, direction, money, a home, support and a community life *before* they are recognised as citizens. And that is true. It should not be necessary to achieve the keys to citizenship; a truly successful community would be one that recognises the citizen in the individual who lacks all those things. But that is not the community in which we live today.

We live in a world where the individual dignity of disabled people is not always recognised and where they have not always been made welcome. In some respects things are definitely improving, but there is much more to be done. It can be argued that only a change by other people, by the community itself, will really help. Perhaps, therefore, disabled people should not have to try to change themselves, should not try to get hold of the keys to citizenship.

But this is not the view that drives this book. Much has been done already by individuals and each time an individual with learning difficulties makes progress in achieving recognition by the community, they do it not just for themselves but they do it for others; and in this way they begin to change the *whole* of society. To my way of thinking it is by each of us doing our own bit, by trying to play a full role as a citizen, that we will each transform the community into a more welcoming place. In the end, if we each carry on behaving as if we do really belong, we will find that we really do belong. Hopefully this book will serve as some kind of guide for those of us who want to make the effort.

This book will not answer every question you might have. In fact if you are a professional or a specialist you might find areas in this book where you feel there is much more that can be said. However the aim of this book is not to try and say everything that can be said on every issue. There are other books and other people you can go to if you become very interested in these things and want more detailed information. I have written this book for all those people who just want to begin with a good clear introductory account of all the main things they need to think about. I have tried to keep the language simple and direct (although I know I often fail) and the book addresses people with learning difficulties themselves as the main audience. I know that some people will not understand this book, but I hope many others will and I hope that in the years to come it is people with learning difficulties and their families who will themselves write guidance books like this.

If you see any mistakes or things that could be improved please let me know by sending me a message by email to simonduffy@mac.com.

KEY ONE: SELF-DETERMINATION

The first thing you need to do if you want to be treated as a citizen is to be recognised by those around you as someone who can be treated as a fellow citizen. This means being someone who counts, someone who has their own voice, their own interests and a life that is genuinely their own. We all want people to treat us as an individual, as a person in our own right.

I will go on to describe how citizenship, in its fullest sense, involves developing six different areas of our own lives. But the most basic requirement for citizenship is that we have 'self-determination'.

The word 'self-determination' is a bit of a mouthful, but it is hard to find a good and simple word for this important idea. The words 'autonomy' and 'self-governance' mean much the same as 'self-determination' but they are just as obscure. So I have decided to use this term, because people with learning difficulties themselves use it.

Put simply, if you have self-determination then this means you are in charge of your own life. If you do not have self-determination then other people are in charge of you. In the United Kingdom there are at least four groups of people who do not have self-determination:

- Children, because they are too young and their parents are meant to be taking care of them.

- Prisoners, because they are being punished and the government takes care of them.

- Some people who are mentally ill, if a doctor thinks they might put themselves or others at risk of getting hurt and then a psychiatrist is put in charge of the person.

- Adults who are said to be mentally incapable, whose minds are thought not to be up to the job of taking care of themselves. In practice it is not always clear who belongs in this group, and it is not always clear who is meant to be responsible for taking care of someone who is said to be mentally incapable.

People with learning difficulties are clearly in danger of being seen as mentally incapable, and are therefore at risk of not being allowed to be full citizens, because the nature of their disability is that they need help, sometimes a great deal of help, with mental things like: thinking, planning, choosing or deciding. I hope to show that self-determination is possible for everyone with a learning difficulty. But first I think I need to explain why self-determination is important.

Why self-determination is important

There are a number of reasons why it is important that people are able to have self-determination.

1 To be legally visible

If you are not treated as someone who can make your own decisions, then there are a lot of things that you are not allowed to do. For example, you may not be allowed to:

- Hold a tenancy or take out a mortgage for your home.
- Control money.
- Get married or have a sexual relationship.
- Control how doctors treat you.
- Enter into contracts.
- Vote.
- Hold legal offices and responsibilities.
- Get a job.

These things matter. They matter because they affect how seriously other people treat you. But more importantly they matter because having a good life can depend upon having the ability to do these things. For example, if you read Peter's Story later in the book (see Figure 27) you will find that it was really important to Peter that he lived in a house that suited him, a house that had to be bought using a mortgage. If there had been no way of getting a mortgage for Peter, then he would have been deprived of a real opportunity for a better life.

2 To be listened to

The second reason that self-determination is important is that if you are somebody who counts, then other people have to listen to what you say. However, if you are not treated as someone whose opinions count, then you will find that people may not listen to what you say, and if they do listen they may not take what you say seriously.

Being listened to is important. It is important because only if people listen to you will you get what you want and need from them. But it is also important because feeling that you are listened to is the basis of self-respect. Nothing undermines how we feel about ourselves more than how others treat what we say and do.

3 To make decisions

The third reason that self-determination is important is that being in charge of our own lives enables us to make decisions. Life requires decisions; even poor decisions are an important part of living. If we can make no decisions then we are stuck and unable to control the direction of our life.

In general, we know what we like and don't like, we know the people we like and the kind of things we like to do. We can't magically get what we want; we need to work to get what we want to achieve. But we can point our lives in what seems to be the right direction for us and we can change the direction of our lives if things don't seem to be going right.

If we are at the mercy of other people's decisions, then we need them to work out what is the right course for our life. Given that it is sometimes quite difficult to know what is the right thing to do in our own life, then obviously deciding for someone else is extremely risky.

So, in summary, we can identify a number of benefits that flow from self-determination. I have set these out in the following table (see Figure 2).

How other people see you	Practical advantages
You are seen as someone with equal rights to others.	You can exercise the same rights as other people.
Other people have to listen to what you say.	You can communicate your needs effectively.
You have an impact on others through your decisions.	You can seize new opportunities and end things you don't like.

Figure 2 The value of self-determination

For those of us who do not have a learning difficulty it is easy to take self-determination for granted. We assume that other citizens should treat us as an equal. We expect that other people will take seriously what we say and that we can make any decisions that are necessary in life. It is our life and we can try to live our life in the way that best suits who we are. We take for granted that we have self-determination and that other people will see us as having that power and treat us accordingly.

But it is too easy to treat self-determination as if it is something that we possess in an 'all or nothing' way. We may think that anybody who is not at risk of having 'mental incapacity' is quite clearly in charge of his or her own life. However, if we think about how we really exercise control over our own lives, we find that self-determination is something that we only exercise to a certain degree:

- We may find that we lack certain rights because of our circumstances; for example, we may not 'have the right' to carry out certain kinds of borrowing if we do not own our own home, we do not 'have a right' to drive a car unless we have passed a driving test.

- We may find that others fail to take us seriously, don't listen to what we are really saying and interpret what we have said in the light of their own stereotypes and prejudices.

- We can become stuck, uncertain of what to do or what to decide. We can become indecisive or refuse to take important decisions.

- We also know that we can lead our own life in a way that is really quite incompetent, which is not true to who we are and which causes us unhappiness and creates stress.

But although we are often not in full and meaningful control of our own lives, this does not mean we do not have self-determination. In order to have self-determination, we do not need to have the maximum level of self-determination. We can still have a degree of self-determination, and we can also improve the level of self-determination we enjoy. We can try and improve our self-determination by either changing the way we behave or by getting other people to help us. We may be able to:

- Improve our effective rights; e.g. by passing a driving test or by negotiating with a bank manager.

- Communicate more effectively; e.g. by finding new ways of making our point, by finding new people who seem to listen better or by getting someone to talk on our behalf.

- Make decisions happen more effectively; e.g. by summoning up our courage or by taking expert advice.

So this is how we should think about self-determination for people with learning difficulties. It is not something that we can decide that this person has and this person does not have. It is something that we can all develop and maximise in our own individual way. My claim is that we can all be in control of our own lives, *to some degree.*

To see how this is possible, to see how self-determination can be developed, we can define the essential things that need to be in place in order to have self-determination. These three things are the following:

Legal status	We must have the legal status necessary to be present in the community and to exercise any of the rights necessary to be a citizen.
A system of communication	We must have a way of communicating our needs and desires to other people.
A decision-making process	We must have a way in which decisions can be made about our lives that maximises our ability to control the course of our life.

These are the three components of self-determination. If they are all present to the maximum degree possible then we are fully self-determining. But even if we need help to have legal status, to communicate, to make decisions or to plan our lives we can still have self-determination. For instance, Stephen Hawking, the famous scientist, needs a voice machine so that he can communicate with other people. But just because he needs help to communicate, this does not stop him from having self-determination.

But how this help is to be achieved will vary enormously depending on the unique qualities of the individual, the nature of their network of family, friends and supporters, the legal situation and the individual's practical needs in their actual circumstances. There is no one answer to how somebody maximises their self-determination. What I will go on to explore are some of the practical steps that can be taken to build self-determination for people with learning difficulties.

How to get self-determination without representation

It is sometimes assumed, wrongly, that just because someone has a learning difficulty they need someone like a guardian to represent them. This is not true in the different countries that make up the United Kingdom. In fact it is rather that the law will assume that you are capable, that you have the same rights as everybody else, until someone proves that you are mentally incapable.

In fact what we might call the law's prejudice in favour of self-determination is even stronger than that. For even if someone proves that you are incapable of making one particular decision, it still has to be shown that you can't make other kinds of decisions or that you can't make that particular decision later. So, in general, the law does not treat people with learning difficulties as lacking any capacity to govern their own lives.

If a court or others decide that you are not capable of making a particular decision, then there may be a need to find you a representative. But I will come on to that issue a little later. You don't always need a representative and if you are seeking to do something without representation then there are a number of things you can do to make sure people recognise that you have the right to make your own decisions.

1 Don't make an unnecessary issue out of capacity

If nobody is making an issue of capacity then don't worry about it unnecessarily. This is such simple advice that it may seem redundant, but it is very important to realise that most people with a learning difficulty can get by without having to put in place any system of representation.

2 Develop self-advocacy skills

It can also help to develop your self-advocacy skills. There are groups of people with learning difficulties across the country who are increasingly self-confident and they give support to their members to learn new skills, express themselves more effectively and to assert themselves. There are also national People First organisations that support those groups and if you don't know how to contact a local group, then one of the national groups will be able to put you in touch with one.

3 Use accessible information

Increasingly organisations, particularly People First organisations, are creating effective books, videos, CDs and other sources of information that are made much more accessible by the use of clear writing, pictures, video and symbols.

There are also computer programmes that you can use to create your own documents and information that you can give to other people so that they know how you communicate.

Some people use what is called a 'communication passport' that tells people what they like and how they communicate. Other people have done something called 'multimedia profiling' where important personal information has been set down on video and in computer programs.

4 Get the right kind of help

Communicating more effectively will only work if the people around you care to listen. Try to find people who are prepared to listen to what you've got to say and are willing to help you achieve what you want to achieve. There is no magical method for getting the right kind of help and there is no one kind of person who is right or wrong to talk to. I will talk more about how you get the right kind of help in Chapter 5.

However, there are a number of typical reasons why some people seem not to be able to listen effectively to people with learning difficulties. These reasons are set out below:

Too busy	Some people just want 'the problem' of your life to go away. They would like somebody else to take responsibility for decisions and they might even prefer it if you went away, perhaps to some 'service' many miles away.
Self-interest	Sometimes people have things to gain from things going a certain way, even if that way does not benefit you. They may prefer to control your money or make sure you have no need to spend your inheritance by putting you in care.
Professional bias	Some people have strong professional interests that mean they tend to think that professionals know best and so only professionals should look after people with learning difficulties. These people may encourage professional solutions when they are not needed, because those solutions make them feel better about what they do for a living.
Over caring	Some people express their love and concern for an individual in ways that are too paternalistic. They want you to be safe, healthy and happy and they are not prepared for you to take the ordinary risks of everyday life.
Ideological commitment	Another kind of bias comes from people who believe passionately in some theory about how disabled people should live. For instance, some people believe that people with learning difficulties should live in special communities. Others think people must live 'normal' lives.

These reasons for not listening are very powerful, and it is important that you try to get help from people who are able to really listen to what you say and who won't sacrifice your interests because of their prejudices or conflicting interests.

Overall then the best approach to keeping your status as someone who can make their own decisions is not to raise the issue unnecessarily. Unless there is a very strong and important reason for raising this as an issue, it is safe to assume that you have the right to make decisions yourself. There is no organisation or person who has the job of going around deciding that some people are not able to make their own decisions. The issue will only arise in certain specific situations and if you manage things properly you may find that you can always be seen as the person making your decisions, even if you have a learning difficulty.

How to get self-determination in partnership

Sometimes the best approach for achieving self-determination is to act in partnership with someone else. This means you are not in the position of being wholly responsible yourself; instead you are a partner with someone else. There is not one way of creating a partnership that will work in every situation. However, there are a number of different partnerships that you can create to achieve specific things.

1 Co-employment

If you want to employ someone to provide you with help, but you don't want the full legal responsibility of being an employer, it is quite possible to co-employ a supporter. This means you make decisions about whom you will employ together with another person or organisation.

For instance, in Glasgow, several people with learning difficulties co-employ their staff with an organisation called Inclusion Glasgow. This means that nobody can be employed unless both the organisation and the person think they are the right person, but also that people cannot be sacked unless both parties agree. This is useful for two reasons. First, being an employer involves serious responsibilities. You need to treat people in the right way or you will get in trouble with the law. Second, it might be useful to have somebody else help you check out who would be a good supporter. You could also co-employ staff with an individual, like a mum or a dad.

2 Joint accounts

Sometimes it is difficult for people with learning difficulties to get their own bank account where they can put their money. If this affects you, then a good way of dealing with this is to set up a joint account with someone you trust. This means your money can be kept separate and safe. However, it is important that the other person or organisation is totally trustworthy.

3 Temporary powers of attorney

A slightly different kind of partnership is involved in giving somebody power of attorney. You can give people power of attorney to do something once, for example, to help you buy a house. Or you can give somebody an ongoing power of attorney to do something like manage your money.

This person acts for you and this can be very useful if there are some things that seem too complicated to understand but you believe a trustworthy friend or family member could understand it for you. Although this person is representing you, he or she is only doing so because you have let them and you can stop them acting for you whenever you want to end the arrangement.

4 Shared ownership

Another way of acting with other people is called shared ownership. This is when you buy something, say a house, together with somebody else. This could be another individual like a brother or sister, or it could be an organisation. Housing Associations, non-profit-making organisations that provide housing, will often help you buy part of your house while they will buy the other part. I will discuss shared ownership more in Chapter 4.

5 Build yourself a circle

One of the most powerful ways of getting partners to help you represent yourself is to gather together a group of friends, neighbours, supporters or other people you trust in a team that will help you. This is sometimes called a 'circle of support' or sometimes just a 'circle'.

There are several reasons why this can be a great way of getting help and I have set some of them down here:

- You can get advice from several different people rather than just relying on one person.
- You are not dependent on just one person for help.
- The circle can develop a team spirit and its members can support each other.
- It can be fun and social.
- It is voluntary and people leave their power and position outside the meetings.

But it is hard work to set one up. It means daring to ask people you like but maybe you don't know too well to give up some of their time to be with you and think about you. It needs time to get going and sometimes the circle will get stuck and people will become demoralised.

There are now several organisations that specialise in promoting circles for people with learning difficulties. The largest of these is Circles Network based in Bristol, but now working across the UK.

How to get self-determination using representation

Although partnership can work well, it will not cover every situation. Sometimes you may find that somebody is not sure that you have agreed to enter the partnership or that you can grant a power of attorney. This might mean that they feel they cannot do what you want, because they don't feel sure enough that it is what you want.

This may seem unfair as it seems to stop you getting what you want. This can happen in a number of situations:

- A lawyer won't accept that you are capable of agreeing to buy a house.
- A Local Authority may not accept that you are capable of managing a Direct Payment for your support services.
- A lawyer may not accept that you can employ or co-employ staff.

These are just some examples of the things you can miss out on if people think you are not capable of really understanding or agreeing to whatever is proposed. Some people feel strongly that this is unfair and the organisation VIA (Values Into Action) campaigns to try and change the law to make it easier for people to keep these rights. However, at this time there is no way round this problem without using some system of representation. This means somebody is picked to look after your interests.

There are lots of ways of doing this and some ways vary even within the United Kingdom. However, there are two very different ways you can get a representative. You can get a representative if this is agreed by consensus or you can get a representative appointed for you by the State.

Agreed by consensus	Appointed by the State
• Family • Advocate • Trust • Support provider • Social worker	• Guardians (e.g. tutor datives, welfare attorneys, financial attorneys) - are appointed by the courts • Hospital consultants - when you go into hospital and they decide you are incapable

Figure 3 The different forms of representation

There is no perfect system for achieving representation. In general it is good if consensus can be reached about who will represent your interests. This has the advantage of being more flexible and easy to change if your needs or situation change. If you go to the courts to arrange some kind of guardian it will be expensive, time consuming and difficult to change. If you go into hospital and the consultant decides that you are mentally incapable (which, is sometimes called being 'incapax'), you are put under the care of the consultant and you have no choice or control over that or anything else.

In the following sections I will discuss some of the different ways you can get representation in more detail.

1 Using your family

It can be a really good idea to use a family member as your representative. Usually your family loves you and knows you well and has regular contact with you. Often you may even be living life happily as part of your family and you may not want to move out of the family home.

Also, if you are lucky, you may have several family members who all have a genuine interest in making sure you are doing well but who are also able to challenge and question each other and make sure that nobody gets complacent and just assumes that you are okay.

Families are also great champions and fighters. If you want to achieve something quite new or different a loving mum, dad, brother or sister is more likely to stick by you and keep fighting than anyone else. Also, families can show a real commitment to helping you develop and play a full part in ordinary life, because families naturally want to bring up their children so that they can become more independent and enjoy all that life has to offer. A good example of a championing mum is given in Michael's story (see Figure 4).

Michael's story

Michael is a young man who lives in a big city. He has a learning difficulty and a strong personality, and he's often got himself in trouble in his local community. But he is also a loving and positive person with a great family.

As Michael grew up his family began to ask for some help so that Michael could attend school, college and become more independent. Unfortunately the only help on offer was a temporary place in a residential home. After Michael attended the first of these homes he escaped back home. So the second place was offered further from home. Again Michael escaped home. The next home was even further away, but again Michael escaped home.

This wasn't really what Michael's family wanted for him anyway. They wanted him to become more independent, but close to home. But there seemed to be no way of making this happen. Eventually his mum heard about a local voluntary organisation that might be able to help her.

Eventually mum and the manager from the voluntary organisation persuaded the local council to do something a bit different. Instead of giving money to different homes, they suggested that the council gave money to the voluntary organisation. The organisation then:

- Helped the family move to a different house, one in which they could create a separate flat for Michael.
- Gave the family a regular income so that they could employ two part-time support workers to help Michael attend College and have a fuller social life.
- Recruited an advocate to spend regular time with Michael and to find out what he was feeling.

Things remain challenging for the family and for Michael; but Michael has continued to develop and remain part of his loving family as he wishes. None of this would have happened without the grit and determination of his mum who persisted in believing that there must be something better possible for Michael and was prepared to fight to make it happen.

Figure 4 Michael's Story

But there are some potential disadvantages when you use a family member as your representative. Sometimes families feel guilt or have other bad feelings because you have a disability. Even though this makes no real sense, it is a real part of ordinary life that many people do not cope well with the existence of disability. If this is the case then you may find family members who want to send you·away to somebody else. This is bad enough; but if the family member also continues to claim responsibility for making decisions on your behalf, this can be extremely difficult.

In other situations families can find it difficult to distinguish their needs from your needs. If everybody in the family is very reliant on benefits then the family might find that their benefits would drop if you left the family home or used your benefits for things that just benefited yourself. Families can also fall out with one another. This can lead to very unhelpful conflict where your interests can get lost.

Finally, mums and dads can sometimes find it difficult to balance their natural desire to see their children happy with the need for their children to develop. Especially for children with disabilities, this latter desire can be repressed and the family can find it difficult to see opportunities for development in their child.

Possible advantages	Possible disadvantages
Families can:	Families can:
Know what you want and understand your needs.	Have bad feelings and negative emotions.
Care passionately and bring energy to get you what you want.	Fail to distinguish your interests from the possibly conflicting interests of other family members.
Bring together several different points of view to debate and decide the best things to do.	Be undermined by internal family conflict.
Really want you to develop.	Be too worried and anxious about what might go wrong.

Figure 5 Using your family as your representative

There are two more points worth making about using your family. If your family is basically a force for good in your life, then you will probably want to include them if you need to. However, you may be able to give them support by also involving an advocate or by using a Trust to balance out your family's point of view. This is explored in more detail below.

You may also find that, while your family are excellent advocates for you, they are always in negative conflict with other important people, like your social worker. This conflict may not be your family's fault. Unfortunately this kind of conflict seems to happen quite often. People, good people, can fall out badly when trying to think about the right thing to do for someone else. Why this happens is not always clear, but I think that partly it is because when people expect to fall out they do end up falling out. They find something they disagree about, spend all their time thinking and arguing about that, forgetting that they probably agree about many more things and that possibly the things they have in common can guide them to work out what is best. I have set out this problem in the figure below (see Figure 6).

Figure 6 Focusing on the wrong things

If you spend time getting people to acknowledge all the important things they agree on and all the important things that need to be improved in people's lives, and then get people to work out what they need to change first, you will often find that people will begin to see that their stereotypes about each other are largely false and unhelpful. This can lead to much more agreement and to everybody working together instead of wasting energy on conflict.

2 Using an advocate

Advocacy, or 'speaking for a cause', can play a vital role in the service system for people with learning difficulties and there is a role for many forms of advocacy. In a way, anybody (including your family) who is representing you should be acting as your advocate. But here I will only describe some of the different kinds of advocate that are usually treated as 'advocates':

Self-advocacy   Some people with learning difficulties are coming together in self-advocacy groups. This is a powerful way for individuals to learn how to speak up for themselves and such groups provide a focus for collective advocacy and campaigning. People who are self-advocates can also be good advocates for other people who have had similar life experiences.

Citizen Advocacy	Citizen advocacy is a way of linking a person with learning difficulties with a non-disabled partner, to form a relationship that allows the non-disabled partner to represent the individual in some aspects of their life. Normally a citizen advocate would be unpaid. This can be very useful, especially if the citizen advocate has had a genuine opportunity to understand who you are and what you would want for yourself.
Parent Advocacy	Many parents come together through national organisations like Mencap or Enable, and increasingly other more local forums such as the Federation of Local Supported Living Groups, and many use other forums to have their voice heard. These groups can provide useful support to families, especially when the family is feeling insecure in standing up for itself. However, parent advocacy is, by its very nature, less concerned with the individual interests of the person with a learning difficulty.
System Advocacy	Where there are complex systems such as the welfare system it is possible to create specialist advisers or advocates who help to support you to use the system effectively. Most Local Authorities have welfare advisers who specialise in providing useful advice about the welfare system. In some areas there are support brokers whose job it is to help you get the best out of the service system. There are also paid specialist advocates who will help you represent your interests to Social Services or other organisations.
Legal Advocacy	Legal advocacy is the form of advocacy most of us are familiar with, that is the use of solicitors and barristers to guide us through the legal system.

The big value of advocacy is its independence. The person who is your advocate is meant to represent your interests to other people - to speak 'for you' to other people - and they do not have any interests that 'conflict' with yours. In theory, this is a perfect arrangement if you need someone to represent your interests. In practice, there can be limitations to advocacy:

- There are only a limited number of advocates available and so they must ration themselves out to those people they think are most in need of an advocate.

- The advocate can focus too much on conflict and not help problems to be properly resolved, leaving you stuck.

- An independent advocate is an advocate who is not involved in your life. But if someone is not involved in your life it can be much more difficult for them to really know you. This means, sometimes, advocates cannot really know what it is they should be advocating.

There is an excellent book on advocacy by Kevin Stone called *To Stand Beside* which gives lots of helpful advice to people who want to be advocates. In this book he describes three different kinds of way of being an advocate:

Being an ally	This means getting alongside people and working along with them to make sure that any changes have the best possible impact on the person who they are advocating for. An ally understands how the system works and tries to use what is good in the system.
Being a defender	This means protecting and defending the person from things that would harm the person. The defender understands the rights of the person and tries to defend the individual's rights.
Being a champion	This means standing up for people and advocating passionately for their cause. The champion has a vision of a better future for the individual and tries to show others how things could be done differently.

He argues that great advocacy involves a combination of these roles and a great advocate knows how to use each different role when the right time comes. Obviously this means the advocate must:

- Understand the system.
- Understand the interests of the person.
- Know how to make things different.

This is challenging for anyone, especially for someone who is not in regular contact with the person they are meant to represent. For this reason it is worthwhile trying to use a team or group of people to help you get the right representation.

3 Using a Trust

In the previous section I talked about what has become known as the 'circle of support' - a group of people who will stand by you and try to help you think about what you want to do and will possibly help you go and get it. I won't repeat the points made above here, but obviously if you can get such a team of people working on your side you will be very fortunate.

But a circle or any group of family or friends can do more than just work with you to support you. They can also form themselves into what is called a 'Trust'. A Trust is a very interesting thing; it is a 'legal person' - a person specially designed to act in your interests. All you have to do to create a Trust is:

- Bring together a group of people.
- Agree the rules the group will work to (called the 'Trust Deed').
- Register the Trust through a lawyer.

A Trust is not the same as a guardian; the Trust does not *take over* responsibility for your life from you. Instead, the Trust is like an extra person who has been artificially created just for the purpose of doing things for you. Trusts can be used to:

- Manage support services to individuals with disabilities.

- Hold ownership of a home or other property.

- Oversee the private funds of the person with a disability.

- Borrow funding for a mortgage.

Another good thing about a Trust is that it can provide a vehicle for decisions to be made into the future without one person having to take all the responsibility. This is particularly important for mums and dads who know that their son or daughter is likely to live much longer than them. If they make all the decisions for their son or daughter then, when they die, they will have no clear way of handing that responsibility over to anybody else. If a Trust is set up, other family members can be invited to join the Trust and can take more responsibility over time.

A Trust can also include non-family members in order to achieve an outside perspective. By inviting a family friend, a trusted professional or someone with a learning difficulty to join the Trust, the Trust is more likely to be able to get a really good understanding of what you need. You might even be able to be a Trustee yourself.

The arrangement of a Trust is not the only way of achieving some of these objectives, but it is a relatively easy one to set up. There is no need to seek guardianship or some other court-managed relationship and it does not involve any onerous responsibilities. A lawyer can provide more information about Trusts and you can also contact the legal services of Enable (in Scotland) or Mencap (in England and Wales).

I have given an example of a simple Trust Deed below where the Trust has been set up to manage a support service; what they call an 'Independent Living Scheme' (see Figure 7). Trusts can be set up with different powers to this and what a lawyer will do is work out with you what you want the Trust to be able to do.

You are strongly advised to seek professional legal advice when setting up a Trust. This example Trust document is meant as a general guide only. (Community Living has published a guide, called *Trusting Independence - A Practical Guide to Independent Living Trusts*, by A. Holman and C. Bewley, which you can order by ringing 0870 7404887).

Not only can a Trust be used to manage funds, it can also be used to purchase things on someone's behalf. An example of this is given in Peter's story (see Figure 27). Peter's Trust purchased a house using a mortgage. However, it is possible, but more complicated for Trusts to charge a rent to the person or to claim for support in paying the mortgage interest. If you are interested in doing either of these things you need to get expert advice.

What a Trust Deed looks like

The following deed is laid out with the information that should be inserted in brackets like this {xx}. Where words are underlined in the deed they are underlined below. Words in CAPITALS in the deed are IN CAPITALS BELOW. Words in (brackets in the deed) are in brackets below.

THIS DECLARATION OF TRUST is made the {xx} day of {xx} 20{XX} by {NAME OF TRUSTEE} of {address of Trustee} {followed by NAMES and addresses of all other Trustees} hereinafter together to be called "the Trustees".

WHEREAS

1   The Trustees wish to provide care and support for {NAME of person benefiting from Trust} of {address of person} who has a learning difficulty by means of an Independent Living Scheme.

2   To that end an Account has been opened at {name of bank} of {address of bank} under the name of the {NAME of person} Trust.

3   Further sums will be credited to the said Account by the {PAYING AUTHORITY} OF {address of authority}.

4   The money in the said Account and any accretions thereto are hereinafter called "the Trust Fund".

5   The Trustees wish to declare the Trusts on which they hold the Trust Fund and the income thereof.

NOW THIS DEED WITNESSES as follows:

1   As from the date of this deed the Trustees shall hold the Trust Fund and the income thereof upon Trust to apply the Trust Fund and the income thereof for the care and support of the said {XX} by making such payments as they in their absolute discretion shall think fit in order to maintain the said {XX} in an Independent Living Scheme.

2   The Trustees shall hold the Trust Fund and the income thereof upon the said Trust until the death of the said {XX} or until he shall cease to be maintained in an Independent Living Scheme whichever shall first occur.

3   Subject to the provisions of clause 2 hereof and to the payment of all outgoings and obligations of the Trustees the Trust Fund and the income thereof shall be held by the Trustees on Trust for the said {XX}.

4   The power of appointing a new Trustee or new Trustees shall be vested in the Trustees or the survivor of them.

5   The number of Trustees shall not be less than two individuals at any time and if at any time the number of Trustees shall fall below two immediate steps shall be taken to appoint a new or additional Trustee or Trustees so as to constitute at least two persons as Trustees.

6   A Trustee shall be entitled to exoneration and indemnity from the Trust Fund for any liability loss or expense incurred under this deed or for any judgement arising out of his or her own wilful and individual fraud, wrongdoing or neglect.

Figure 7 A Sample Trust Deed

4 Using your support provider

For lots of people with learning difficulties who use services it is their support provider who is treated as their representative. This can be okay; it can be quite useful if your key worker is given the job, say of sorting out your benefits, and in theory the key worker will be managed by and be being checked by somebody else in the organisation.

However, support providers are only another set of human beings and they have their own limitations. In the following table I have set down some of the good things and the bad things about using a support provider as your representative (see Figure 8).

Good things	Bad things
Support providers should be organised so that decisions can be made quickly.	Support providers may be tempted to cover up anything that will make their organisation look bad.
Support providers should have a management system to check out what is going on.	Support providers can be bureaucratic and can leave some decisions in the hands of managers you don't even know.
Support providers should be able to take calculated risks.	Sometimes support providers can be confused about who exactly is doing what - this can lead to big delays and confusion.
Support providers should have some expertise about how the service system and the benefits system work.	Support providers may look at things from the point of view of the whole organisation first.

Figure 8 Using your support provider

In practice, if you use a support provider and you need a representative for lots of important decisions, then you will probably find that it works best if you ask the support provider to act on your behalf for many things. However, if possible you will try and do some of these things as well:

- Get the support provider to be clear about who in the organisation can make what decisions and try to get day-to-day decisions made by people who are working closely with you.

- Look at the support provider's policies to check whether they give good guidance and encourage people to think about what is in their real interests.

• Get the support provider to meet regularly with a family member, a friend or an advocate so that they can check for you that things are going the right way.

5 Using a social worker

Social workers (sometimes known as care managers) play a crucial role in helping to represent people when everything else has broken down and no one else is available to represent someone's interests properly. In fact part of their job is to work out whether you need a representative and if so then they must work out who is the best person to play that role. If they cannot find anybody, then that becomes their role.

However, having a social worker as your representative should only be a short-term solution to any problem, because a social worker's job makes it very difficult for them to play that role for a long period. This is because:

• Social workers have to think about lots of different people at any one time.

• Your social worker may not have the time to get to know you well.

• Social workers are trained to keep a professional distance that may make it difficult for them to get to know you well.

• Social workers sometimes also have to think about managing budgets and that job can sometimes conflict with the job of looking after your interests.

Work with your social worker to find a better system of representation so that the social worker can organise, fund and monitor the support you get without needing to represent your interests over a long period.

6 Using a guardian

The last kind of representative that I want to talk about is the 'guardian'. In fact the law has a lot of different names for different kinds of guardians but I will not go into those details now. In general, a guardian is somebody who has been appointed by the court to be your representative in some or all matters.

The major problem with guardianships is that they are fixed and inflexible, and if one starts to go wrong then you have to rely on the courts to fix it rather than just getting people to alter the decision-making arrangements as they go along. The major advantage of a guardianship is that if people are disagreeing radically, then getting the courts to fix it at least makes sure some decision has to be made.

In general it is therefore best to avoid the expense and uncertainty involved in going to court. However, if you think that this is something that you should think about you will need proper legal advice.

VIA have written a number of interesting books that discuss these issues further and propose a very different system for how people could be supported to make their own decisions with varying degrees of support. They call this system 'Supported decision-making'.

The last representative that I mentioned above is the consultant of a 'mental handicap hospital'. I do not think that this needs to be treated at length. Nobody should be in a hospital just because they have difficulty making decisions. Even if you are in hospital, there is no reason why your doctor is automatically the best person to make decisions about what is right for you. This is just an old-fashioned practice from the days when people with learning difficulties were put out of their communities and into the hands of the institutions where they were expected to live out their days, under the rule of the staff, until they died. It should go without saying that this is unacceptable and that nobody should be forced to live in these institutions any longer.

How to get people to listen to you

Even if, technically, you are legally visible this is not enough to achieve self-determination. It is not enough for everyone to agree that:

- You are in control of your own life, or

- You have a partnership with somebody else to make decisions, or

- You use a representative to make decisions.

Even if everybody agrees that you do use one of these methods to make decisions (or you use some mixture of these methods), this is only the beginning. You also need people to *listen* to what you are saying. And people can listen to you even if you do not speak using ordinary words.

To explore how this is possible I am not going to try and describe all the different ways people have found of communicating. Instead I am going to talk more generally about how communication works and I hope to show that for all of us, no matter how difficult communication might be, communication is possible.

Communication involves three things:

- A means of expression

- A willingness to take what has been expressed as meaning something

- A shared language in which something is being expressed

1 Find a means of expression

People use all of the following things to communicate:

• Spoken words	• Written words	• Pictures
• Actions	• Symbols	• Photographs
• Body movement	• Sounds	• Hand signs and gestures
• Art	• Computers	• Communication equipment
• Eye movement	• Following requests	• Refusing to follow requests

If you can use any of these methods of expression (or the many others that I am sure are possible), then you can make the first step to communication. It is very important to realise that even the smallest form of expression can convey meaning. Possibly as much meaning as the spoken or written word can convey.

For instance, Jean Dominique Bauby wrote *The Diving Bell and the Butterfly* after suffering a sudden and severe stroke. After the stroke Bauby was able to move only his left eyelid. Unable to write or speak, he composed passages of his book in his head and then dictated it, letter by letter, to a helper who painstakingly read the alphabet until he picked a letter by blinking his left eyelid. This story should inspire us to remember that anything, even the smallest flicker of expression, can be used as the starting point of communication.

2 Find a willing listener

What Bauby needed next, and what anybody needs if they are going to try and communicate, is a listener who is genuinely wanting to listen and will treat what is expressed as potentially meaningful. This means that before we worry about how we communicate we need somebody else to be present who genuinely wants to 'hear' what we have to say.

This is not a skill; it is an attitude. It is the attitude of being positively interested in what someone might be saying and if you have that interest you will assume that what the person is expressing is meaningful.

So in the case of Bauby, it is only when somebody said to themselves, "That flickering eyelid, perhaps it means something; perhaps he is trying to tell us something." It is only when we assume that someone is trying to communicate that we can listen to them in the right way, actively looking for their meaning.

Reasons why people listen	Reasons why people don't listen
They love you.	They don't like you.
They want your world to be better.	They think they already know you and what people like you need.
They are interested in you.	What you are saying may be too difficult for them.
They are interested in what you want.	It is easier to carry on doing things the way they have always been done (even if it doesn't suit you).
They want to learn.	They think they have nothing to learn, they are experts.

Figure 9 Why people listen

So if you are someone who does struggle to communicate then the most important thing is to try and identify people who really want to listen. These may be people close to you, but if they are not then you will have to seek out people who seem genuinely to care.

Most of all it is unlikely that people who are simply being paid to work with lots of different people who do not communicate in standard ways will be in the best position to help you communicate. They will be stretched between many different people, all of whom will be trying to communicate with them in different ways. You will be better off trying to communicate with people who see you often and who are thinking mostly about you when they try and listen.

I have set down some of the reasons people do and do not listen in the table in Figure 9.

If I am allowed to be a little bit poetic, we could say that love comes before meaning. When we care we can seek out a meaning in what is expressed, however it is expressed. But if we do not care we will not find the meaning.

3 Build a language of communication

Once we have someone trying to express themselves and someone trying to listen, trying to understand, then it becomes possible for a language to develop that will make communication possible. For Bauby that language was just an extension of the French language he knew already, to which he and his helper added the system for picking out letters. But we can have languages even when we do not know a formal written language.

A language is a system of communication where the means of expression is connected to what is meant. Examples of different kinds of languages are given in the table below (see Figure 10).

This expression	in this language	means
Waving your hand	in body language	hello or goodbye
Giving someone a hug	in body language	I really like you
A red traffic light	in UK Highway code	stop
− − − . . . − − −	in Morse Code	help!
Moving your hand away from your mouth	in British Sign Language	thank you
Saying 'merci'	in French	thank you

Figure 10 Different languages

Now it may be that you do not use spoken or written English. However you may well be able to learn another language. Some people with learning difficulties have learnt how to use British Sign Language (BSL) or a system of signs and symbols called Makaton.

But even if you can't learn a language that has already been made up, it is still possible that you and the people around you can learn your own personal language. The name for your personal language is your 'idiolect' and if you can get somebody to understand your way of communicating then you have built your own language together with that person.

This might seem a very difficult thing to do. But in fact it is very easy and it works for everybody who can find even the simplest way of expressing themselves.

For instance, most people have some way of letting other people know that they are happy or unhappy. In fact people who know you really well and who care about you will know a lot about how you communicate and it can be very useful to gather that information together. A useful way of gathering that information is provided by the following chart (see Figure 11).

(1) When this is happening	(2) and you do this	(3) we think it means this	(4) and we should do this

Figure 11 Communication Chart

If your friends think hard they will be able to identify bits of your behaviour that seem to be telling them something (column 2) or things that they think you are communicating (column 3). If they then write these things down your friends should be able to think about when you use these ways of communicating (column 1) and what should be done when you do (column 4). It is important to remember when you are doing this that:

- We can communicate differently with different people.

- We might want people to respond in different ways.

- We can change how we communicate in different settings.

- The same bit of behaviour might mean something different in a different setting.

An example of a real communication chart is given on the following page:

When this happens:	and Jacob does this:	We think it means:	and we should do this:
Jacob is doing something	hums	Jacob is happy	Encourage and praise Jacob
At the day centre or at the Hostel	batters things	Jacob is feeling bored	Find something interesting for Jacob to do
At the day centre or at the Hostel	batters things	Jacob is feeling inquisitive	Find safe things for Jacob to explore or play with
At the day centre or at the Hostel	throws his dinner	Jacob is upset	Comfort and reassure Jacob
At the day centre or at the Hostel	throws his dinner	Jacob does not like the food	Find food Jacob likes or let him know you will do so soon
At the day centre or at the Hostel	throws his dinner	Jacob is not hungry yet	Let Jacob eat later
At the Hostel	throws his dinner	Jacob is feeling inquisitive not hungry	Let Jacob eat later and explore things now
Jacob has just done something to upset you	Jacob puts his head down	Jacob is sorry	Leave Jacob for a short while and then reassure him
Jacob is in the company of young women	acts aggressively towards women	Jacob likes you a lot	Give Jacob something else interesting to pay attention to
At the Hostel	slaps you	Jacob wants your attention	Give him positive attention - like a hug
At the Hostel	grabs at his trousers	Jacob wants to go to the toilet	Support Jacob to go to the toilet
At the Hostel, in the living room	heads for living room door	Jacob wants to go to his room	Support Jacob to go to his room
At the day centre or at the Hostel	acts aggressively	Jacob doesn't like being told what to do	Rethink your request
At the day centre or at the Hostel	acts aggressively	Jacob wants to go to his room	Support Jacob to go to his room
At the Hostel	tugs your hair	Jacob likes you	Give Jacob an affectionate cuddle
Jacob is told his food will be made later	grabs at other people's food	Jacob is fed up and wants immediate attention	Encourage Jacob to be patient and to wait
Jacob is being encouraged to try new food	grabs at other people's food	Jacob doesn't want to try the new thing	Find a different meal for Jacob
At the Hostel	Pushes the food off his plate	Jacob is experimenting with food	Encourage Jacob to keep food on the plate

Figure 12 Jacob's Communications Chart

How to make your own decisions

I began by claiming that self-determination was important to all of us, that none of us would like to give away control over our own lives. I then claimed that self-determination was also a complicated thing; not something that you just have or do not have but something that you can have to a greater or lesser extent. I then broke down what self-determination meant into three parts:

- Being legally visible – being accepted by the community as someone who can make decisions.

- Being able to communicate – finding a way to express yourself to others.

- Being able to make decisions – finding a way of making choices in your life.

In the sections above we found that there are many ways of being accepted by the community as being able to make decisions on your own behalf. We have also discovered that there are many ways that people can communicate. We will now turn to the question of how decisions can best be made in a way that maximises the individual's control over their own life.

In fact, by considering the things we explored above we should already be clear how decisions should be made by, with or for someone with a learning difficulty. For each important area of decision-making we should try to identify who should make decisions and how the person should be involved in the decisions that affect their life.

1 Who should make decisions?

Is it clear who will make key decisions on your behalf? It is not helpful to be unclear about decisions. This can often lead to unnecessary conflict and confusion. Every effort should be made to make decision-making clear and focused on keeping you at the centre of your own life. Having nobody to make decisions on your behalf can sometimes be worse than having imperfect decisions made on your behalf.

But when people make decisions on your behalf they potentially have the power to make decisions that go against your best interests and abuse you, either emotionally, financially, physically or sexually. One of the best ways of protecting yourself from abuse is to make sure you only give decision-making on your behalf to people you trust. Good things to think about are:

- Involve people who know you well and care about you.

- Involve different people, not everybody with the same kind of relationship to you.

- Don't give people control over decisions where they could benefit from not acting in your best interests.

- Have a wide network or people around you to look out for your interests; don't just rely on one or two people.

The fundamental principle here is that decision-making should be left with you unless there is a good reason to believe that this would lead to significant harm to you or others.

2 How to stay in control

Whether or not you make the final decision about choices in your life, there are lots of ways you can stay involved and can influence any decision that is made.

First of all, making decisions can depend upon having the right information available to you about the choices you are making. If you have the right information available then that choice is an 'informed choice'. Tools that can be useful in making decisions include the following:

- Have pictures or photos to represent the choices on offer.

- Have words or writing setting out the choices on offer.

- Describe the good and bad parts of each possible choice.

- Talk to people who have made the choice before.

- Watch videos or listen to stories.

- Try things out before making a bigger commitment, if possible.

- Use computers or other forms of technology to communicate.

It is possible for people to get impatient with you if they think you should be making a certain choice. But it is important to not let yourself be pressured unnecessarily. In the story below we can see how helping people have the right information can be a vital part of helping someone make the right choice for themselves (see Figure 13).

Second, not only must you be able to get information, you must be given the chance to express your preferences in your own way. This is not just about getting to know your system of communication. It is also about the way you like to think about things. For some of us to express our preferences we may need to be:

- Talking to the right person - sometimes we like to go away to think about something, sometimes we like to sit and chat with friends.

- Taking the time to think about things – some of us like to 'sleep on it'. It is very important that you do not allow people to rush you into choices when you are not ready to make them.

- In the right place to decide – for most of us it is easier to shop for clothes in clothes shops, but some of us like to shop from catalogues and try things on at home.

- In the right mood to make decisions – sometimes we can be so upset by something that we want people to take a bit more responsibility for us for a short time.

- Planning on how you will decide - If you get anxious or confused when put on the spot, you might also want to have a plan about what you will do when you have to make a certain choice.

- Asked in the right way – nobody likes to be asked too many questions at one time. It is also helpful for people to break complicated choices down and think about what the key issues are from your point of view.

In Ann's Story below I give an example of how we must not just think about how someone communicates. We must also respect how they need to make particular decisions (see Figure 13). The fundamental principle is that, whoever is going to make the final decision, you are entitled to influence any and every decision that is going to affect your life.

Ann's Story

Ann lived in a large residential home. She had lived there for many years and thought it a great improvement on the hospital where she was forced to live before. But Ann had started to think that maybe it was time for her to move on, to find a place of her own. In fact her supporters agreed; in their view it was 'time for Ann to move on' and they were eager that she make the move.

The problem was that Ann kept changing her mind. Some days she thought it was a good thing to move. Sometimes she thought it was a bad thing. Her supporters even got a little frustrated: "The problem with Ann is she can't make up her own mind." So the supporters asked an independent person to come and plan with her to 'help her make her mind up'.

The first thing the independent person did was spend a little time with Ann to learn a little bit more about how she lived. One thing that struck him was that Ann was a great shopper; she often went into town and hunted for bargains with her friend Mary. But her supporters were describing her as someone who couldn't make up her mind; that seemed odd.

So the independent person suggested to Ann that she get together with people she liked and trusted and that they would think about all the different things she could do. Then they could list all the good and bad things about each choice and write it all down. So this is what they did and the facilitator took away all the words and pictures and then drew them up as a shopping catalogue. Ann was then able to look at and think about all her choices, in her own time.

Six months later Ann decided. She and her friend Mary were going to live in a flat together. This was not what people were expecting, but Ann and Mary were determined. They persuaded their supporters and they persuaded their social worker, and in a few months they had their own flat where they lived together enjoying a new level of freedom and responsibility, together.

Ann (and Mary) had made a decision, but at their own pace and with the information they needed.

Figure 13 Ann's Story

3 Make a Decision-making Agreement

It is important to remember that it is your life and that as much as possible you need to control your own life. This is because you have a right to control your life and to make your own decisions, but also because you will usually know what is right for you.

Even if you need some help to make decisions, it is still possible for you to remain in control of your own life. What is important is that your plan helps people understand how you can still make decisions. It may be useful to write it down in the form of a 'decision-making agreement'. One example of a decision-making agreement is set out below (see Figure 14).

Important decisions in my life	How I must be involved	Who makes final decision
Setting my household budget and claiming benefits	I want my mum to talk to me about my benefits and my budget when it is set up – my supporters will need to know from my mum what is in the budget.	Mum
Buying my food at the shops	One of my supporters should help me to make a shopping list before we go – at the shops I will pick and choose everything.	Me
Managing my support funding	I want my mum to talk to me about my support funding and help me understand how it is used.	Mum
Collecting my benefits	I will collect my own benefits and put them in the bank and handle my money in accordance with the budget – with reminders from my supporters about what money I have available.	Me
Recruitment of new staff	All staff will be recruited according to a person specification drawn up with me. I will meet all staff before appointment and nobody will be employed who I do not like.	Mum

Figure 14 Decision-making agreement

This is just an example and you may find you need to detail more or less than this depending on your circumstances.

An agreement like this should demonstrate that real thinking has been done to involve you properly in small and big decisions about your life. There must be really good reasons why you are not making a decision on your own behalf. If there is any doubt then other people should always presume you have the right to decide yourself.

So, if you are at risk either from people deciding things on your behalf or if you are at risk from not being involved, you could use a decision-making agreement. This can make clear:

- All areas where you can clearly make your own decisions.
- How you will be supported if you need help with your own decisions.
- Who will help you with which decisions.
- Anybody who will make decisions on your behalf.
- How they will continue to involve you in those decisions.

This brings us to the end of this chapter. I have tried to explain why self-determination, the ability to be in charge of your own life, is an important idea. But I have also tried to show that we do not treat people with learning difficulties as lacking self-determination just because they need help to make decisions. There is much we can do to ensure that people can play a full part in society and can make decisions for themselves.

Of course it is right that we should worry that people are not being quietly abused in the name of self-determination; for it is possible to dress up decisions to make them look as if the person is involved, when really they are not. But this is no reason not to improve someone's control over their own life. We all know that we can be unduly influenced by others, be abused by others or misled by the wrong information. But this does not mean we want less information or no advice or help. Instead we simply need to think about how to get better information and improve the help we receive.

But even if we can help someone to achieve self-determination this is only the beginning of citizenship. The next step is to live our own life, to have a life with its own unique sense of direction. So what I will go on to discuss is direction and how we get it.

Organisations that can offer advice on promoting self-determination

BILD (British Institute of Learning Disabilities) Campion House, Green Street, Kidderminster, Worcestershire DY10 1JL, tel: 01562 723 010,
website: www.bild.org.uk

Circles Network, Potford's Dam Farm, Coventry Road, Cawston, Rugby, Warwickshire CV23 9JP, tel: 01788 816671,
website: www.circlesnetwork.org.uk

Enable, 6th Floor, 7 Buchanan St, Glasgow, Lanarkshire G1 3HL,
tel: 0141 226 4541,
website: www.enable.org.uk

Family Carer Network, c/o Home Farm Trust, Merchants House, Wapping Road, Bristol BS1 4RW, tel: 02380 653 833,
website: www.hft.org.uk

Making Decisions Alliance, c/o Mental Health Foundation & Foundation for People with Learning Disabilities, 7th Floor, 83 Victoria Street,
London SW1H 0HW, tel: 020 7802 0300,
website: www.makingdecisions.org.uk

MENCAP National Centre, 123 Golden Lane, London, EC1Y 0RT.
tel: 020 7454 0454,
website: www.mencap.org.uk

Mind, The Mental Health Charity, 15-19 Broadway, London E15 4BQ,
mindinfoline: 08457 666 163,
website: www.mind.org.uk

Multimedia Profiling Project, Aylesbury Vale Healthcare Trust,
Manor House, Bierton Road,
tel: 01296 504353,
email: michael.kennally@avchc-tr.anglox.nhs.uk

National Forum of People with Learning Disabilities, c/o PO Box 2100, Shoreham-by-Sea, West Sussex, BN43 5UG
website: www.nationalforum.org.uk

Values Into Action, Oxford House, Derbyshire Street, London E2 6HG,
tel: 0207 729 5436,
website: www.viauk.org

Useful reading

Bauby, J.D., *The Diving Bell and the Butterfly,* Knopf (New York), 1997

Bewley, C., *Choice and Control,* Values Into Action, 1998

Stone, K., *To Stand Beside,* Stone & Associates, 1999

KEY TWO: DIRECTION

The second key to citizenship is to have direction. To be able to make decisions is just a first step. Beyond being able to decide, we also need a sense of *what* we are trying to achieve, our direction, a plan. We might say that the first step to citizenship is to have control over our own life, but the second step is to give that life direction.

This may not seem obvious. However, we all know what it means for someone's life to have purpose. And most of us know what it feels like to lack direction. Purpose is not about having every step of your life planned out. Nor is purpose about achieving some final goal. Purpose is about finding your own path, a path that feels right to you and developing a lifestyle which offers you satisfaction and personal fulfilment.

But having personal direction, having a purpose is not necessarily easy and it is quite common for any one of us to find that our life has gone adrift; we find ourselves unhappy or trapped (maybe in a relationship or in a job or in a service), but afraid to change or uncertain what to change towards. One word that is commonly used for the process of giving your life direction is to plan. There are lots of good reasons why planning is important in life. Here are just a few:

Planning helps us change things	We can all get stuck in a rut; sometimes we don't even know we're stuck in a rut. This is especially likely when we need help from other people for things in our everyday life, because we have to fit our life around what is easy or convenient for others. To get out of a rut we need to work out what we would like to do instead. Working that out is the same as having a plan.
Planning helps us feel more confident	When we don't know what we want or how to get it we can feel worried or frustrated. Sometimes we can even get angry if things are not how we would like them to be. Planning can help us work out what we can change and can give us a way of making change happen. It feels good to have a plan.
Planning helps us work with others	Not only is it important for us to have a plan, but it is also important that other people know the plan too - so they can change what they do and be more helpful. Most people want to help and do the right thing, but often they don't know what that is and they will carry on doing the same old thing, just because they are not sure what else to do. Plans help everyone act differently.
Planning makes things real	Sometimes we have hopes or dreams that we may not even talk about to others. But if we start to plan to achieve our goals then we have to work out how we can make things happen. Sometimes it is easy to make changes;

sometimes it is very hard. But easy or hard, we can only make our dreams come true if we work out what to do, and do it. Plans help us work out how to get what we want.

This does not have to mean doing anything fancy or complicated. Good planning just means working out what you want to do with your life and working out how to make it happen. But although this is fundamentally a simple idea there is now a term, a piece of jargon, which is used to describe this simple idea; that term is 'Person Centred Planning'.

Now it may seem surprising that we need to use such a long-winded term to describe something as simple as working out what we really want to do with our lives. But there is a reason why people came up with this special term. They did it because sometimes the kind of planning that professionals in human services do with the people they serve is not really based on what the person really wants or what is really right for them. People write 'care plans' or do 'assessments' but these are not 'centred' on the person. Instead they reflect the needs and assumptions of human services.

Frequently the kind of planning done by human services is focused only on things that services think are important, like 'learning how to shop and cook' or 'learning how to control one's temper'. And the planning is done in a way that suits the service, not the individual.

In order to explain the difference between these two approaches, I have set down some of the contrasting characteristics of these two types of planning (see Figure 15). The difference is very real and anyone who has experienced both styles of planning can quickly recognise the difference.

Of course it is not the term 'care plan' or the term 'assessment' that makes something service-centred. People can write a good Person Centred Plan, but call it a 'care plan' just as they can also write an awful plan and call it 'Person Centred'. In fact, what frequently happens in human services is that a new term like 'Person Centred' arises out of an attempt to say something new or to make an important distinction that had been missed before.

But this new term will soon be taken over by the service world. Soon everything will be called Person Centred, because it is a new buzz-word. It is much easier to re-label something 'Person Centred' than to genuinely change the focus and nature of human services. I know of one excellent organisation so disillusioned by this process that they now refuse to use the term 'Person Centred', but instead they simply try to show that they are Person Centred by their actions.

Seen in this way, Person Centred Planning should then be regarded as an alternative approach to planning: not planning *for* individuals but individuals planning for themselves, possibly with the help of others. However, making this shift towards being Person Centred is difficult. For it is not usually a negative attitude or ignorance that stops people from looking at things from the

Service Centred Care Planning and Assessments	Person Centred Planning
Focuses on what's 'wrong' with someone and tries to fix it.	Focuses on the person's gifts and tries to use them.
Starts by thinking about things that are priorities for the service.	Starts by focusing upon what is most pressing for the individual.
Gives most emphasis to the professional judgements of clinicians.	Gives most emphasis to the voice of the person themselves and to those who love them.
Uses the plan to identify services for the individual to make use of.	Plans so that people can make the best use of their local community.
Provides an opportunity for powerful professionals to offer people places in their existing services.	Provides friends and family the opportunity to think about ways they or people they know might be able to help.
Fits itself into existing bureaucratic and management systems.	Fits itself into the lifestyle and pattern of acquaintances of the individual.
Seeks a consistent formula that will allow consistency between different cases.	Works best when it is refreshed by different approaches and experimentation. There is no standard frequency, no standard group who must be involved, no standard format.
Tends to be held in places where professionals feel comfortable, e.g. offices and clinics.	Meetings are held when and where is most convenient for the person.
Other people are planning for the individual and ideally enabling the person to be involved as much as possible.	The individual is in charge of planning their own life and is involving others as they see fit.

Figure 15 Service Centred vs. Person Centred Planning

perspective of the person, it is a whole range of factors that inhibit and limit our imagination:

Life is not easy	We can all get stuck sometimes, unable to find direction or unable to see how to achieve what we want. For this reason many of us have found Person Centred Planning useful in our own lives, as a way of achieving focus and goals that better reflect who we really are.
Support is powerful	If our life is in the control of others then decisions are made without reference to us or to people who are important to us. There are lots of other demands placed upon services, staffing requirements, satisfying the Local Authority, living up to the organisational objectives, meeting the competing needs of different individuals. All of these demands create lots and lots of objectives that quickly crowd out the chance that we will hear what the individual really wants to do.
We all make assumptions	If we rely on others to support us we are vulnerable to their assumptions about what is important for us. We can all feel that we know best what is right for somebody else to do. In ordinary life this is a fairly harmless weakness. But where we have control over someone else's life then our prejudices are potentially dangerous, especially when they are not balanced by any alternative view or perspective.
We can become defined by our support	If our life is in the control of others, then we can easily lose our sense of having our own life and our own community. Instead we become defined by their habits and practices. We need our own set of connections, interests, friendships and family ties. When we are isolated from those things we end up grasping hold of anything that can give our life some purpose. If we end up 'in' human services, it is all too easy for the real world to disappear and for life to become focused only on the artificial world of support in which we've found ourselves.

Why Person Centred Planning works

At the heart of Person Centred Planning is the belief that every single individual has their own life to lead, a life that is right for them. Sometimes it is difficult to work out the best thing to do and sometimes we need people to help us work out the best thing to do. Person Centred Planning is the process of helping someone work out the right thing to do, for himself or herself. At its simplest it involves:

- Understanding yourself.
- Setting yourself goals.
- Working towards those goals.

1 Self-understanding

If your plan is really going to be your plan then it needs to be based upon some understanding of the unique individual that you are. There are many different ways of understanding who you are and so there are many questions you can use to uncover who you really are. Here are just a few:

- What works for me? What doesn't work for me?
- What are my everyday positive rituals and routines? For instance, how do I like to get up in the morning? How do I like to spend my Saturdays?
- What would my ideal holiday be like?
- What are my dreams and hopes for the future?
- What are my nightmares and fears?
- What does a good day for me look like? What does a bad day look like?
- What would an ideal week look like for me?
- What are my gifts and skills?
- What makes me feel safe?
- What are my strengths and needs?
- What would I do if I won the Lottery?
- What do people like about me?
- What do people respect about me?
- What do I want to achieve in the next five years?
- What is my life story so far?
- What would I like people to say about me at my funeral?

All these questions, and many more, share the purpose of trying to help us reflect on our unique identity or purpose. Some are more mundane than others. Some are grand and ambitious. But all of them take for granted that we each have our own unique identity, one that may even be lost or hidden, but an identity that is truly our own. Each question works in a different way to uncover something true about us. But there is no perfect question. Each question has its strengths and each has its weaknesses and they work better in some circumstances than in others.

For instance, one family who were planning with their son about where he should live, struggled to think about his housing situation as he left a long-stay hospital. Their imaginations were constrained by grim accounts of community care and the assumption that he must live in some council housing estate. But when they were asked to imagine that they had won the lottery and, in their imaginations, to build a perfect house for their son they knew exactly what was right for him. They pictured a four-bedroom home, close to his sister, by the seaside and in a location that would give privacy and easy access to long country walks. Moreover, after 18 months of hard work this was the house that their son was able to live in. In fact even if they had not been able to achieve all the details contained within their dream for their son, it may not have mattered too much. What really helped was that the family began to see that there could be real opportunities that might really suit the unique individual who was their son.

2 Setting goals

Once you have some sense of who you are then you are able to begin the process of finding a direction for yourself, a plan or a goal for your future. Nobody can tell you what goals you should have. But there are some things that tend to be very important and they are set out in the following list:

- To make everyday choices.
- To have people treat me with respect.
- To take part in everyday activities.
- To have friendships and relationships.
- To be part of my local community.
- To get the chance to work.
- To take part in important decisions about my life.
- To have people listen to my family's views.
- To be safe from harassment and abuse.
- To get help to stay healthy.

This list is meant to help you think about the kinds of things that are important in life. It cannot tell you what is important to you. Although it may be important to achieve the kinds of goals set out in the list above, it is not helpful to state those goals for yourself in that way. Instead be as specific and as realistic as possible about what you want to achieve. In the following table the general goal has been made more specific by thinking about real things that an individual really wants to achieve (see Figure 16).

Good questions to ask yourself about your goals are:

Do your goals make sense?	Your goals should reflect the real you. They should be your goals and it should be easy to understand why your goals follow from what you understand about the real you. In this way your goals will be genuine, things you really want to achieve.
Are your goals real?	If it is impossible to tell whether your goals have been achieved, then you will not know whether you have achieved them or how far you've yet to go. Goals should not be vague or intangible.
Are your goals achievable?	You should set goals you think you can achieve. This means that if you have big ambitions then you may be best setting goals that are achievable first steps towards

your ambitions. You should also only include as many goals as you can reasonably achieve. If you set yourself impossible targets you can fail to see the progress you are making and lose faith in yourself.

General goal	Examples of specific goals
To make everyday choices	I will decide what meals I am going to have in my own home. I will choose how to spend my own money. I will choose what clothes to wear.
To have people treat me with respect	People will learn how to communicate with me. I will get personal care in private. I will get the chance to become more independent.
To take part in everyday activities	I will do my own housework. I will pursue my own hobbies at home. I will have interesting activities to attend.
To have friendships and relationships	I will have friends that I see often. I will spend regular time with my family. I will get married to my boyfriend/girlfriend.
To be part of my local community	I will get to know my neighbours. I will attend the local college. I will help out in my local community.
To get the chance to work	I will get a paid job. I will do voluntary work. I will make friends with my work colleagues.
To take part in important decisions about my life	I will decide where I live. I will decide who supports me. I will decide how I live.
To have people listen to my family's views	My family will be involved in important decisions. My family will know how to stick up for my rights. My family will get information about services.
To be safe from harassment and abuse	I will not be bullied or insulted. I will not be hurt or abused. My property will be safe.
To get help to stay healthy	I will keep fit. I will get good health checks. I will have a local doctor who I trust.

Figure 16 Examples of specific goals

None of this means you should be a martyr to your goals. Your goals exist to serve you; they are to help you have direction and purpose, something to aim for. There is nothing to stop you changing your mind as you learn more about yourself. Nor should you feel that you must constantly try to make big changes in your life. There is nothing to stop you setting goals that are about keeping alive parts of your life that you value.

3 Making the plan happen

But planning is more than just defining our goals. Planning should always lead to action. We first begin by trying to understand; understanding our own dreams, hope, needs or values. Often it is best to try and understand without worrying too soon about what your goals will be. Thinking about the goal can distract us from understanding. Then there is a time to set goals, to decide what it is you will try to achieve. Our goals should be as clear and realistic as possible, because clear goals help us determine our course of action.

Finally you must turn your ideas into reality, you must make the plan happen. Often people can achieve much more than they realise but it doesn't happen just by setting goals. Instead you must act. But often we need to do more planning to work out *how* to achieve our goals. This kind of planning is called action planning.

There are a number of things that can help you do good action planning, and what you will need to do will depend on the nature of the goals you have set yourself. Some of the things you may need to do are:

- Recognise the realities of your present situation: How are things now?

- Recognise the things that are fixed at the moment: What money is available now? What skills do people have now? Who is around who can help now?

- Identify opportunities: Is there a new funding source available? Do you share an interest with a friend? What local resources are available?

- Prioritise - decide what's most important to you today. Don't try to do everything, do the most important and urgent things first.

- Assess risks - be clear what frightens you. Work out plans that enable you to overcome your fears or reduce the risks.

Using these methods you must finally reach a point where you can identify clear action steps. The following principles are useful to bear in mind when developing an action plan:

Clarify what needs to be done   Make sure everybody understands *what* must be done as the next step to make the plan happen. Sometimes it is easy to see what needs to be done to make a plan happen. Other times it is difficult. When it is difficult it can be useful to:

- Work out all the steps you need to get you where you want to be.

- Get more information.

- Talk to somebody who has done it before.

- Make sure that you at least make the next step towards your plan.

Often you find you need to think more about how something is going to be achieved before you can decide what is going to be done.

Find somebody to help you do it

After you are clear what needs to be done then you can work out who should do it. It is vital that you are clear *who* is responsible for making something happen:

- If something is everybody's job usually nobody does it.

- If someone needs help to do it then also agree who will give that person the help they need.

Agree when it will be done

It is also important to agree with the person *when* the next step will be done. Remember that it is up to the person who is going to do it to say when it can be done. There is no point asking people to do things that they cannot get done when you need them done.

Decide when it will be reviewed

The most important part of any planning is to make sure that you know how you will check out what has been done. Often it's a really good idea to plan a meeting where everybody can get back together and discuss what has happened. It is also important to ask yourself and your friends how you find the planning is going. Maybe you will need to change *how* you plan.

How to use Person Centred Planning in practice

Person Centred Planning is not the name of some special therapy or treatment for disabled people. It is actually just a long name for the quite natural process that we all go through, for better or for worse, at different times in our lives. It is hard to generalise too much about what makes for good Person Centred Planning; for different individuals not only want different things they also think about themselves and their lives in different ways. However we do know a certain amount about what makes for successful Person Centred Planning and some of the things you need to think about as you begin to plan:

Involve the right people

It is good to involve all the important people in your life when you plan, both so you can get their ideas and so you can involve them in anything you decide to do. People you might involve might include:

- Family.

- Friends.

- Professionals who you know that you trust.

- Your supporters.

It is not good to involve people who won't help you develop your plan. Some of the people who you shouldn't involve include:

- People you don't like.
- People who hardly know you.
- People you don't trust.
- People who don't understand you well.

If there is anybody like this who thinks that they should help you plan, then get help to make sure they do not get involved in your plan. Sometimes there are also people, like doctors, who might not be good people to plan with but who have useful information that's needed for your plan. Make sure you or your supporters get the information from these people without involving them in your plans too much.

Plan at the right time

Planning is something that we often do without even thinking about it. For example, if we are planning to catch a bus we need to get ready by knowing what bus we want and having the right change for our journey. But planning for our life is a much bigger thing that we don't do often, if at all. However, it can be very useful when the time is right. These are some of the times when it's good to plan:

- When you've got to make big decisions, like what support you want.
- When you feel stuck in a rut.
- When you need new challenges or things to achieve.
- When you are unhappy about your life.

Some times are not so good for planning and you may not want to plan or you may want some other people to plan for you for a while until you are ready. These are some of the times when it is not so good to plan:

- When you've got too many other things on your mind or you feel in crisis.
- When you've got some practical problems that must be sorted out first before you can plan.

It is okay to let other people plan for you sometimes, but it's best if this is just for a short period and that everybody tries as hard as possible to make sure you can be involved in the future. It's your life and nobody else's.

Find a good place to plan

Think about where you'd like to sit, talk and think. All of us are different. Here are some of the different places people choose to plan:

- In their home.
- In an office.
- In a hotel.
- In the pub.
- In the car.

Some places are not so good for planning. So don't pick places where:

- You might bump into people you don't like.
- You will feel uncomfortable or inhibited.
- You might have no privacy if you need it.

Use the right equipment

It can be really helpful to use some special equipment or stationery to plan. For example some of these things might be useful:

- Pictures or photographs.
- Coloured pens.
- Flip-chart paper or other large bits of paper attached to walls with masking tape.
- Computer equipment, including scanners and clip-art.

Set some rules in advance

It is often really handy to set out some rules for planning. What these rules are can vary but if everybody agrees to them at the beginning it can make everything go much easier. Here are some rules that you might want to set:

- Remember that this planning is about me, don't get distracted and talk about things that are not relevant to my life.
- Don't try and solve problems too early, everybody should listen to the whole story first before making suggestions about what to do.
- Be honest but also positive, don't run anybody down.
- Don't talk about me as if I'm not there.
- Keep any confidential information private and don't share it with others without my permission.
- Talk to me, not to each other.
- Assume that everyone has a positive contribution to make.

- Use respectful language at all times; if I'm an adult don't talk about me as if I'm a child.

- Try to use language that everyone can understand.

1 Using Person Centred Planning Tools

Sometimes it is helpful to have a clear plan or process to help you do Person Centred Planning. That is, to get a good plan, sometimes you need to think about things in a particular order and in the right way. These structured plans for planning are called 'Person Centred Planning tools'.

There are a number of these structured processes that you can use to help yourself to plan. Different individuals have developed them in slightly different contexts and they are becoming increasingly well known within the UK. I have set out four of the main Person Centred Planning tools in more detail below and there are training courses and booklets that describe all of them in more detail:

PATH: Planning Alternative Tomorrows with Hope

PATH was developed by John O'Brien, Marsha Forest and Jack Pearpoint. It is a graphical model for planning that helps people find direction and build strength. The central idea is that you identify your 'dream' (which can be as unrealistic as you like) and then you use this dream to set yourself realistic goals. It is a really good thing to do when:

- You are stuck and have nothing to look forward to.

- You have people who care but they don't know how to help.

- You have a sense of a better future but need help to say what it is.

- You like the idea of a planning event for you and your friends and family.

It takes approximately two hours to carry out a PATH. Ideally you would have two trained people facilitating the PATH, one writing things up on paper and one asking questions. It's normally a fun process and it is very good at getting people from a vague sense of something better to precise action steps. But it is not, by itself, good at solving complicated problems and for some people the idea of thinking about their dream can be too threatening.

MAPS: Making Action Plans

MAPS was developed by John O'Brien, Marsha Forest, Jack Pearpoint, Judith Snow and David Hasbury. It asks a series of questions which individuals can use to develop a plan of action. It explores the person's history, dreams, nightmares, gifts and other positive qualities. After exploring these questions you then ask yourself what you want to change in your life. MAPS is particularly useful if:

- You need to see where you've been in the past to think about what's next.

- You want people to think about your gifts and strengths.

- You want people to look at your fears.

In order to do the first exploratory part of the MAPS process, you need to set aside about an hour and a half and you really need to get some good people together to help you think about your gifts (as few of us like talking about our positive qualities). When it comes to solving problems and changing the things you want to change, this part can be done in different ways and at different times and the MAPS process has no special trick to help you.

ELP: Essential Lifestyle Planning

Essential Lifestyle Planning was developed by Michael Smull and Susan Harrison. It is a powerful means of gathering information about what is important to you now. It uses this information to help you work out what is not working well in your life and what important things you are not getting. It also helps to work out what other people need to do to support you well and when, if at all, they should do things for you to keep you healthy or safe from harm. It is an excellent tool to use if:

- You feel poorly supported at the moment.

- You don't feel others understand your preferences.

- You have special routines or rituals that you want others to know so they can support you better.

- It's difficult to let people know what is important to you by speech alone.

- There is confusion about how best to keep you safe or healthy.

Ideally you would find someone trained in Essential Lifestyle Planning to help you develop your Essential Lifestyle Plan. The planner can meet several people at once or can hold interviews with key people in your life. At best it will take one day of meetings or several days of interviews to gather the necessary information. It will also take up to one whole day to write down the information and organise it. This information is not even a plan yet, although it should contain guidance for your supporters on how best to support you. The planning begins once the information is gathered and how best it is achieved will depend upon the issues raised.

PFP: Personal Futures Planning

Personal Futures Planning was developed by Beth Mount. It is a flexible set of questions and graphical maps that can be used to build up a sense of who you are and how you would like to live. Personal Futures Planning is much less structured than the other approaches and offers a range of questions or approaches suitable for different problems. It is a really good thing to use when:

- You want to get more involved in your local community.

- You want to improve your network of friends and family.

- You want to plan for something really specific, like moving house or leaving school.

There are a number of books you can use to learn more about Personal Futures Planning and some people have been trained to use it. Personal Futures Planning can be done in half an hour or it can take much longer, depending on what you want to use it to explore. Although it is less well defined than the other tools, its great strength is its flexibility and its attention to the opportunities that are created by life and our relationships with others.

Make up your own plan

These different Person Centred Planning tools are all excellent. But you may find that there are better ways of asking the questions you want to ask yourself or involving others. Some people have used their own special ways of getting a plan. Here are just a few examples:

- Planning and playing bowls at the same time.

- Turning the plan into play-acting.

- Making a game out of the plan.

- Interviewing people instead of having meetings.

There are no rules about what process to use. Just think about what you want to find out and then ask yourself what might be a good way of finding the answer.

2 Getting help to plan

If you feel that you or someone you care about would benefit from having a Person Centred Plan, but you are daunted by the idea of doing it there are a number of things you can do:

Get training

Sign up for training courses in Person Centred Planning. There are many available across the country; many of them are free or highly subsidised for people with learning difficulties and their families.

Read the books	There are many more detailed accounts of how to do Person Centred Planning than are available in this book. Most of the important books are listed at the end of this chapter.
Meet up with others	Possibly the most important way of learning about Person Centred Planning is to find ways of meeting up with other people who are trying to do the same thing. From them you can gain confidence, practical support and ideas about how to do it.

You can also get help from other people. There are already a number of people trained in Person Centred Planning; some Local Authorities have encouraged people to learn about Person Centred Planning and some providers have become skilled at using the planning techniques. In particular you are likely to come across a number of key groups who may know something about Person Centred Planning:

Service providers	Use your common-sense. If the organisation tells you it is good at Person Centred Planning but it actually offers identical services to all the people it serves, then it is unlikely that they will really be able to help you think about what you need. However, some service providers aren't like that. Ask around and get the opinion of other people with learning difficulties and their families.
Care managers	Some care managers are skilled at using Person Centred Planning techniques. However, remember that care managers also have the job of trying to ration limited resources and to fill services. Good care managers don't let this distract them. But some care managers cannot really step outside their role as representative of the Local Authority.
Support brokers	Occasionally you might find that there are support brokers or other independent advocates who are skilled in Person Centred Planning. This is possibly the ideal kind of help, as support brokers are independent of both the Local Authority and service provision. Unfortunately there are only a few support brokers presently available.
Human Service Consultants	There are a number of organisations that specialise in offering training, development and consultancy for people with learning difficulties. They are expensive for individuals or families to commission directly but will sometimes do work for free. You can try to ask for their help anyway or try to pressurise the Local Authority to commission one. However, although these individuals can provide useful pieces of one-off work they are unlikely to be able to provide long-term support.

The most important piece of advice that I would give you is to make sure you *just do it*. Don't be overawed by all the different planning tools, questions and ideas about the process. Start by planning, get together with some people that you care about and who care about you and think about what you want to do. If you are doing this on behalf of someone who doesn't communicate with words, then try to think about what they would say. Then write down your plan - if you can, even try to cost your plan. Just the fact of having a written-down plan gives you immense authority when dealing with others when you want to involve other people.

For instance, one family in North Lanarkshire were given the chance to make use of a new system of self-directed support. They were told what kind of things a support plan would need to include and offered help to do it. But the family decided they would just try and do it themselves. The next weekend the young man with a learning difficulty sat down to Sunday lunch with his mum, dad, brother and sister and they decided what should be in the plan. The dad, who was good with figures and computers, then wrote it down. When the social worker arrived the following week she was amazed; she was given a plan that would have taken her several weeks to develop. In my experience there are many more people and families like that, who can do much more for themselves if they are encouraged and given some kind of framework to work to (see Figure 17).

Support Plans in North Lanarkshire

North Lanarkshire has developed a system of self-directed support that has given families and individuals the chance to manage their own support services or pay service providers to manage the support services. However, in order to be able to receive the funding for such services, there must be a support plan in place. The support plan can be done in many different ways and with different methods of support, but it must answer the following seven questions. The guidance gives the following summary of what is required:

1 Who are you?

The plan must be about you, the real you. Somebody who loves you or cares about you would be able to recognise that this plan was about you.

The plan will not be agreed if your real personality, interests and lifestyle are ignored and you are treated as a stereotype.

2 What are your plans for the future?

The plan must set out real and measurable things that will have happened in the future so that it is possible to see whether the plan is working or not.

The plan will not be agreed if you just said that you wanted to be happy or that you wanted your needs met but you didn't explain what that meant.

3 What support will you need to do what you plan?

The plan must say what kind of support you are going to use to do what you want to do.

The plan will not be agreed if you have no idea how you are going to use your funds to get support.

4 How will you stay healthy and safe?

The plan must say how you will make sure that you are not going to be in any great risk of coming to harm and also how you will keep other people safe from harm.

The plan will not be agreed if you or others are at great risk of harm but you've done nothing about it.

5 How will you stay in control of your own life?

The plan must say how you will stay in control of your own life. This means looking at what decisions you will make and, where other people make decisions for you, how they will make sure that you are involved and that you would agree to them.

The plan will not be agreed if it looks like others are making decisions for you when you could reasonably make those decisions yourself.

6 How will your support be managed?

The plan must explain how any support you pay for is going to be organised. This means saying who is going to manage it and how you will sort out the payment of salaries or other necessary practical arrangements.

The plan will not be agreed if it is unclear who is responsible for what, and that you are not doing everything that you must do by law.

7 What will your support cost?

The plan must set out what the support service will cost for a year and what money will be needed for the following two years. This must be within an amount agreed by North Lanarkshire Council.

The plan will not be agreed if the plan does not say how much the service will cost or if the service costs more than the amount that has been agreed.

Figure 17 Good practice in planning

Why Person Centred Planning is useful

In conclusion I think it is worth stating what Person Centred Planning can achieve, but also clarifying its limits, what it won't achieve by itself.

1 It is positive

Person Centred Planning is a positive experience, one that can provide you with a chance to think about your strengths and interests and then build on these. In general, optimists make the best problem-solvers and if you look positively at who you are and what you might achieve then you find that you can be successful, sometimes well beyond your expectations.

2 It is inclusive

Person Centred Planning is designed to include others and to work in a non-professional, non-judgemental way. People who for years have felt overawed by professional decision-makers suddenly find that they have a role to play or are even right at the centre of things. Also the process encourages other people to get involved, it encourages people to join in your efforts to achieve your goals.

3 It is realistic

When Person Centred Planning is done well it is highly realistic. Although it may involve asking you to put reality to one side for a moment, as part of the process of dreaming, it has to return to reality. One family referred to an Essential Lifestyle Plan as their 'Bible' because the plan presented a positive, real and totally comprehensive document that really described their son. Another mum describes the Personal Futures Plan that was done with her and her daughter as the first document actually to describe her daughter properly, as the young woman she is. But it is not just a matter of being realistic about the person but also realistic about the world and the constraints that actually operate. There is nothing person centred about escaping into a fantastical image of the future and never returning to the hard question of how to make things better, for real.

4 It is respectful

Person Centred Planning is respectful. It is done at your pace, where you want and it involves people who you trust and value. This is not just about being nice. If someone is planning for you in a way that does not involve you, respect you and which gives a lot of power and authority to people you neither trust nor like, then you will not be motivated to achieve the goals of the plan, no matter how 'good' they are supposed to be for you. Human services are full of well-intentioned care plans that will never be achieved because they rely on the commitment of the person themselves, but the person never agreed to the goals in the first place.

5 It is powerful

Person Centred Planning is powerful. It draws together different people, creates a shared image of the future and it gives people the permission and clarity they need to head towards that goal. It doesn't always lead exactly where one intends. New learning happens, people change their minds, but it helps people take control of their lives in a powerful alliance with others.

For anyone who has really experienced good Person Centred Planning, the experience is unlikely to be forgotten and will not be mistaken for care planning or anything else. But like any new idea, Person Centred Planning has been subject to misrepresentation, distortion and misuse. Increasingly the term is being used without reference to the experience and values that underpin it and certain myths have grown up that may damage the reputation of Person Centred Planning. So it is also important to remember what Person Centred Planning is not:

Not a solution for every problem

Person Centred Planning is not an antidote for all the stupidities of human services, the injustices of the world or every problem in life. Person Centred Planning does what it says it will do, it helps people plan in a way that is centred upon them. But planning is not magic. A business needs a business plan, but having a business plan alone won't save the organisation from bankruptcy.

Not identical to any Person Centred Planning tool

Another myth that has grown up is that doing good Person Centred Planning is a matter of religiously applying the Person Centred Planning tools; as if these tools were set in stone as opposed to being just ideas and questions that have been organised by other human beings. But when people lose sight of why they are planning and begin instead to focus on 'doing a PATH' or having an 'ELP', then they are not being person centred. Being person centred means working out how you want to plan; and if you don't really want a PATH or that won't ask the right questions for you, then you need to do something different.

For example, Tony is a man who loves to party but hates any kind of planning meeting. For Tony even the most elaborately designed planning session is a horror, a place where from his past experience people came together to say negative things about him. But he sure can party. He loves games, food, music and being the host of the event. So holding a party has proved to be a really effective way of getting some things done, including recruiting his supporters. Planning is now done by creating games that can be played without anyone having to go into 'meeting mode'.

It is not the next trendy thing

The cynical response to Person Centred Planning is that 'we've seen it all before' and that after a few years these terms and ideas will be replaced by the next latest replacement for Individual Care Plans. Of course there is something true here. There were certainly lots of people doing good Person Centred Planning before anybody coined the term and no doubt the term 'person centred' will go the way of all things and fade into history at some point. However, I do not think Person Centred Planning is just some fad or trick; in my experience it is simply the very real effort of helping an individual work out what they want to do in a way that is true for them.

It is not the only kind of planning possible

One further myth is that Person Centred Planning is such a good thing that it is the only kind of planning you are allowed to do. However, this is a confusion. If you are running an organisation you still need to look at things from the perspective of the organisation and that means you need to do business planning. For example, one organisation who had invested heavily in planning in a person centred way with those it served was struggling with how to close a residential home in this way. What they found was that they had to combine their person centred work with a project plan for closing the home. In fact that it was only by being non-person centred for a time that they could successfully be person centred later.

Alternatively, if you are a family, then you may need to think 'as a family' and this may involve organising things that involve a certain kind of compromise between conflicting individual needs. Compromise and mutual accommodation is part of life; what is unacceptable is that people's lives simply become subject to the needs or hopes of others, not that other people might have some influence over our lives.

Moreover, there are even times when planning 'for' someone can become necessary. There are, in my experience, circumstances where someone's behaviour may be endangering themselves or others and that therefore clear planning needs to be done about that person, for that person and without that person. For example, Jane is a lady with learning difficulties and someone who has had a severe drinking problem. After moving from hospital to her own home she had a moment of crisis where she returned to drinking, and her drinking habit was so extreme that once begun it did not stop and everything in her life ground to a halt. Now planning *with* Jane in these circumstances, particularly as her team had to develop strategies on how they would deal with her more difficult forms of behaviour, was not really possible. The final plan for Jane involved doing things Jane did not immediately like. However, the effect of this plan was to give Jane much more security and control over her life.

It is not just for people who talk

One of the most damaging myths is the view that Person Centred Planning is okay for people who can communicate what they want to some degree, but it is no good for people who cannot communicate. This is false and if you believe it you exclude so many people from the opportunity to have a good plan for their life.

There are two reasons why this is false. First, everybody can communicate. No matter how severe their cognitive disability, people find a way of conveying what they like and what they don't like. Someone may not be able to answer a direct question, but as long as somebody in their life cares about them then it is possible to understand how they would like their life to be. Essential Lifestyle Planning is a particularly good tool for building out of that kind of knowledge a coherent account of somebody's preferences.

Second, it's okay to listen to the dreams of others. If you want to listen to somebody who cannot communicate with words easily there is nothing wrong with listening to the people who care about that person. Nobody can be a perfect advocate on that person's behalf, but perfection is not necessary. It is much better to encourage people to dream on someone's behalf than never to develop a good plan because we don't know what the person really wants. A much better way of compensating for the natural bias that a person who cares brings, is to find other people who care and to get them to talk to each other and work out together what would be right for the person.

Real Person Centred Planning creates a sense of purpose to life and, for the people you meet, it helps them understand the meaning of your life. This is what we look for in each other and it provides the second key to citizenship. For when we recognise that someone has their own purpose, their own reason for being here, then we can recognise that they too have their own life to lead, one that is worthy of respect.

Organisations that provide training in Person Centred Planning

Circles Network, Potford's Dam Farm, Coventry Road, Cawston, Rugby, Warwickshire CV23 9JP, tel: 01788 816671, website: www.circlesnetwork.org.uk

Edinburgh Development Group, John Cotton Business Centre, Sunnyside, Edinburgh EH7 5RA, tel: 0131 476 0522, website: www.edg-sco.org

Helen Sanderson Associates, 34 Broomfield Road, Heaton Moor, Stockport SK4 4ND, tel: 0161 442 8271, email: helen@sandersonassociates.co.uk

The Foundation for People with Learning Disabilities, Sea Containers House, 20 Upper Ground, London SE1 9QB, tel: 020 7803 1100, website: www.learningdisabilities.org.uk

National Development Team (NDT), Albion Wharf, Albion Street, Manchester M1 5LN, tel: 0161 228 7055, email: office@ndt.org.uk

New Possibilities Ltd, Yvonne Smith, 86 Drayton Road, Kings Heath, Birmingham B14 7LR, tel: 0121 242 3605, email: newpossibilities@blueyonder.co.uk, website: www.newpossibilities.co.uk

NWTDT (North West Training & Development Team), The Globe Centre, St. James Square, Accrington, BB5 0RE, tel: 01254 306 850 website: www.nwtdt.com

Paradigm, 8 Brandon Street, Birkenhead CH41 5HN, tel: 0870 010 4933, email: admin@paradigm-uk.org, website: www.paradigm-uk.org

Red House, Ty Coch, Llanfihangel, Llanfiyllin, Powys SY22 5JD, tel: 01691 648909

SHS Trust, 1A Washington Court, Washington Lane, Edinburgh EH11 2HA, tel: 0131 538 7717, website: shstrust.org.uk

Useful Reading

Bradley, V., Ashbaugh, J. & Blaney, B. (Eds), *Creating Individual Supports for People with Developmental Disabilities - a mandate for change at many levels*, Paul H Brookes, 1994

Cole, A., McIntosh, B. & Whittaker, A., *'We Want Our Voices Heard' Developing New Lifestyles with Disabled People*, Policy Press, 2000

Department of Health Social Services Inspectorate, *Planning for Life; Developing Community Services for People with Complex Multiple Disabilities*, Department of Health, 1995

Mount, B., *Capacity Work,*. Communitas Publication, 1995

Mount, B. & Zwernik, K., *It's Never Too Early, It's Never Too Late,* St. Paul, MN, 1988

O'Brien, J. & Lovett, H., *Finding a Way Towards Everyday Lives - the contribution of Person Centred Planning,* Lithonia, GA: Responsive Systems Associates, 1992

O'Brien, J. & O'Brien, C. L. (Eds.), *A Little Book About Person Centred Planning*, Inclusion Press, 1998

People First, Manchester and Liverpool, *Our Plan for Planning*, Manchester People First, 1997

Sanderson, H., Kennedy, J., Ritchie, P. & Goodwin, G., *People, Plans and Possibilities - exploring Person Centred Planning,* SHS, Edinburgh, 1997

Smull, M. W. and Harrison, S. B., *Supporting People with Severe Reputations in the Community,* Alexandria, VA: National Association of State Mental Retardation Program Directors, 1991

O'Brien, J. & Forest, M. with Snow, Pearpoint & Hasbury, *Action for Inclusion - how to improve schools by welcoming children with special needs into regular classroom,* Toronto, Inclusion Press, 1989

KEY THREE: MONEY

If you have achieved the first key to citizenship then you have some control over your own life. If you have achieved the second key to citizenship then you have an idea about what you want to do with your life. But now you have to make things actually happen. This means you need to get other people to do things that you need them to do.

There are basically two reasons why people will do things for you. People will help you either because of love or because of money. Of course when I use the word 'love' I mean it in a very broad sense, not just when we are 'in love' with someone. Here are just a few of the different ways love affects how we behave:

- We do things for the people we love.
- We do things for friends that we like.
- We do things for people we are fond of.
- We do things out of the love of God and our fellow man.
- We do things because we think they are right.

Perhaps love is not the right word to cover all of these different things, but it is the best word I can come up with. What is important here is to see that if people feel love for you (in any one of these ways) then those people may do things in ways that suit you and what you are trying to do with your life.

Love is a wonderful thing and without love nothing would be possible. But I am not going to talk more about love until we discuss the last key to citizenship: 'A community life'. At this point I want you to see that however marvellous love is, it has one weakness for someone who wants to be a citizen and who wants to take charge of their life and lead it as they see fit. You cannot control love.

You cannot control how people feel about you and you cannot control what they do about those feelings. So love, for all its strengths, will not always help you live life as a citizen - as your own person. As well as love you need money.

Again, money might not be the best word here. But I am using money to cover all of these kinds of things:

- Cash.
- Money in the bank.
- Stuff you can swap.
- Tokens, vouchers etc.

All of these things will enable you to get people to do things that you want them to do. For if other people believe that they can gain something for themselves by selling you something, providing you with a service or swapping something with you then they will do it. This is called *'exchange'*: you do something for me and in return I will do something for you.

The important thing for us about money is that it gives us some control over our lives. Money helps us to achieve our plans; it helps us to take the right direction. So in this chapter I want to explore two things:

- How you can get money.
- How you should use your money.

How to get money

1 Earning money

The way most people get money is to earn it by doing a job. Some people do this by running their own business, but most do it by being employed to work for somebody else or an organisation.

Now if you are an adult with a learning difficulty there is absolutely no reason why you should not think about getting a job and earning some money. At the moment few people with learning difficulties have jobs (the government estimates somewhere between 4 and 10% of people). But things are improving and people with learning difficulties, no matter how significant their disability, have been able to get some kind of work and earn some money. For instance, one young woman, who has a job, tells her story below (see Figure 18).

A Message from Rebecca Westwood

Hi there, my name is Rebecca Westwood. I am 21 and I come from Chelmsford. I would like to tell you about supported employment and what I do. I have had a job for quite some time and I have a lot of fun. It makes you have something to look forward to and it can be good for someone with a learning difficulty that finds it hard to get work. I like working, it is fun and you get paid for it and you can do a morning or an afternoon.

When I am at work, I answer the telephone, take messages and work on the computer. I also do photocopying and answer the door. This is the first time in my life that I have worked. It is fun and it does me some good. It makes me feel good because I am learning something different all the time.

Apart from working at the Ling Trust office, I do some presentation work at conferences and I enjoy it a lot. I joined the Ling Trust team at the Paradigm conference in Birmingham. We did a role-play on how Social Services sometimes treat clients. We all got on very well and achieved what we set out to achieve.

We are the people with disabilities; we have a voice that needs to be heard. I believe that all people should have the right to stay where they want to stay and no one should ever be moved out of their home. My advice to you is GO FOR IT! Don't ever waste an opportunity. Grab it with both hands and make the most of it. Never ever look back.

Figure 18 Rebecca's Message

Getting a job is not always easy but there are several ways you can go about trying to find work:

2 Finding a job on your own

Getting a job is about finding someone out in the world who needs what you have to give. Ideally then you are trying to do two things:

1 Work out what gift, talent or skill you want to use to earn money.

2 Find someone who needs that talent or gift and get them to believe you are the right person for them.

Many books have been written about how to find the right job. One of the best of those books is called *What Color is Your Parachute?* by Richard Nelson Bolles. But some of the key steps to finding work are set out below.

First Step   Identify the kind of job you want to do:

- Do you have a dream job?
- Is there a good job that is similar to your dream job?
- Do you have a skill you enjoy using?
- Do you have a gift that others might enjoy?
- Is there a place you love being?
- Is there an activity you love doing?

Any one of these questions might give you the ideas you need to look for the right job for you. But, whichever idea you come up with, don't be afraid of setting your sights on something. Even if things don't quite work out as you plan, you will achieve nothing if you do not set your sights on a particular kind of job or place of work.

Second Step   Identify who offers those kind of jobs:

- Are the jobs advertised in newspapers and if so which ones?
- Do you or your family, friends or supporters know anybody doing similar work or employing people in such work?
- Who are the biggest employers in your area?

This is about doing research; finding out who is around and offering the kinds of jobs you are interested in. Remember to ask around, use your contacts and don't be afraid to just ask to meet people and ask for more information. Sometimes it is just by going to meet someone to ask about how you would get a job that you make the key contact that leads to the job you are looking for.

Third Step   Find out what employers are looking for in the people they employ:

- Would you benefit from any special qualifications?

- Would you need experience?

- Do you need to write them a letter or draw up a CV?

- Do they do interviews and, if they do, what kind of things do they ask?

Fourth Step   Get to meet your possible employer:

- Do you need to apply for an advertised job and fill out an application form?

- Can you just set up a meeting with a possible employer?

- Should you just write a letter to the employer?

Some organisations work in a very structured and rigid way when it comes to employing people. Some organisations are quite different and are much more flexible. The best thing is to get your foot in the door and meet people face to face. It is much easier for people to say 'no' to a letter than it is for them to say 'no' to your face.

Fifth Step   Show what you have to offer. In any meeting or interview you want to give yourself the best possible chance of showing what you can do. In particular you want to show that you have:

- A good positive attitude: Let the employer know that you are keen to do the work and you want to do it well.

- Experience: What have you done before that shows what you've got to offer? It doesn't need to be previous work experience.

- Skills: What skills have you got that you can offer to the employer?

While attitude alone will not get you the job it is probably the most important thing. Skills can, with time, be taught or help can be given and experience will only come with time, but if you do not have the right attitude this will have a bad effect on your work and your work colleagues.

Sixth Step   If the employer is interested in you then there are a number of things you will want to try and negotiate with your employer:

- How much you will be paid.

- What hours you will work.

- What support you will get from your employer and your work colleagues.

- What support (if any) you will need to bring with you.

- What changes or adaptations will need to be made to help you work effectively.

Remember that if the employer wants you, it's because he wants you to work well. So don't be afraid to talk about help you will need or changes that might be needed.

Also remember that as well as being a good way of earning money, work is also a good way of making friends. So don't cut yourself off from the other employees and if you are bringing a supporter to help you in your work, make sure that everybody knows that it's your job and that people need to talk to you and help you, rather than your supporter.

Seventh Step Review and change your job as you develop as a person. People rarely stay in the same job for ever or stay with the same employer, so you will need to think about how it's going and how things could be changed or improved. But wherever possible talk to your employer about what you are looking for. Maybe they can help you make a change.

To many of us all of this may seem impossible. However much people would like a job, there is a frequent assumption that people with learning difficulties are incapable of work or that they are only able to do certain kinds of work, like gardening or cleaning. However, there is plenty of evidence that all people with learning difficulties, even people who seem to have very significant disabilities, can work in a wide range of jobs. Some of the jobs people already hold include:

- Actors
- Musicians
- Office workers
- Shop workers
- Mechanics and garage workers
- Carers and supporters
- Classroom assistants
- Trainers
- Consultants
- TV Presenters
- Gardeners

- Factory workers
- Removals
- Cleaning and housekeeping
- Authors
- Artists
- Salespeople
- Restaurant workers
- Farm workers
- Cooks
- Building work

In fact the list of possible jobs is endless. So don't limit yourself to certain kinds of jobs just because they are the only jobs that people 'like you' are able to do.

3 Use a Supported Employment Agency

A Supported Employment Agency is a special kind of organisation that helps people with learning difficulties get and keep jobs. If you are lucky there may be an organisation like this in your local area and if you are really lucky they may be able to help you, although this normally depends on both:

- Getting a referral, possibly from your social worker.

- Meeting their 'eligibility criteria' – that means that you have the qualities that they have decided you must have in order for you to be a priority 'case'.

If you can get to use a Supported Employment Agency then this can be really useful, because Supported Employment Agencies will normally help you by providing one or more of the following things:

Vocational Profiling	This is a fancy way of saying that they will help you think about the jobs you want to do and the skills and experiences you can use to help you get a job.
Job Coaching	A Job Coach is a special kind of supporter who specialises in helping people in their jobs. They would help you by doing parts of the job with you or by offering you help if you got stuck.
Systematic Instruction	This means working out all the different bits that make up any job and helping you do each bit for yourself over time.
Job Identification	Finding employers who might be interested in employing you to do the work you would like to do.
Negotiation with employer	Help to negotiate the right deal with your employer and help for the employer to work out the right way to support you in your job.
Developing Natural Support	Help to think about how you can become a full member of the team, make new friends and not become isolated at work.

This is not just for people who are quite independent already. Work is an option for anybody who wants to do it, for if people get support already then there is no reason why they cannot be supported to work. For example, Ian's story shows that people can be supported to take on jobs that many would never have expected to see them doing (see Figure 19).

Ian's Story

Ian had lived in hospital for 20 years. No one thought he would be able to get a job. He spent most of his time in hospital sitting in a corner with building bricks. He has limited speech and was not credited with any skills. An organisation called LEAF (Life, Employment and Friends) started to work with Ian and his supporters to try and improve his life. He now has a job as an administrative assistant, helping with mail shots, franking, and general office duties. Initially Ian had to be supported in all his work but now he completes many tasks unaided. He started one morning a week but was soon asked to work three because he was so reliable and flexible. He is now regarded as one of the workforce and has his own PIN number to enter the building. Ian gets paid for his work and delights in reminding his boss if his wages are late.

Figure 19 Ian's Story

Supported Employment Agencies are a great way of finding work and they have had great success. But remember if you can't find an agency to help you, do not give up. There is much that you can do for yourself or with the help of friends, family and supporters.

4 Use your network to get a job

In some countries it is taken for granted that you get jobs through family and friends. But in the UK we sometimes forget how effective our personal network can be at helping us find a job. If you are looking for a job, think about talking to your family and friends about it.

Also remember that even if they can't help they may know somebody who could – so ask them to think about asking people they know. This can extend the number of people who might be able to help you by a huge degree. If you have 30 people in your network of family or friends and each of those people has 30 people in their network of family and friends, then if you ask your network to use their network you can contact up to 900 people. Also if you can get them to contact people in their networks, you can contact up to 27,000 people – that is the size of a small town.

5 Use Government Programmes to find work

As well as the Supported Employment Agencies that are often funded by Local Authorities, there are a number of national programmes and agencies that are meant to help people find work. These include:

- *Workstep* – a government-sponsored employer of disabled people.
- *The Working Age Agency* – the new version of job centres that are meant to help everybody get a job who wants one.
- *New Deal for Disabled People* – a national project to improve access to work for all disabled people in the UK.

It is unlikely that these programmes will be able to help everybody in every area. But it is worth trying to find out what is going on in your area and using whatever services they may have.

6 Overcoming the benefit trap

The biggest problem in finding work is the problem of benefits. Many people are put off looking for work because they are worried they will lose benefits like Income Support or Housing Benefit. This is a huge problem as the modern benefit system has been designed in a way that can make it financially unattractive to work too much. There is no easy way round this problem at the moment and it will take major changes in national policy to change the way the benefit system works. However, if you want to work you can do the following:

Come off benefits   This is a good solution if you can get a job that allows you to work enough hours and pays you enough money. Sometimes this is not possible.

Work a small amount	Typically the government allows disabled people claiming benefit to earn a small amount before it affects their benefits. You need to get advice about what this amount is from a benefits expert and then make sure you earn no more than that amount.
Get special benefits	Because the government knows that the benefit system discourages some disabled people from working, it is often tinkering with it to make it easier for people to earn and claim benefits. Special benefits are put in place that you claim for while you work. You will need to take good advice from an independent benefits adviser or a Supported Employment Agency before using these benefits, as they are usually quite complicated to claim for.

7 Inheriting money

Another way of getting money is to inherit it from your family. Although only a small number of people benefit from inheritance at the moment, it is likely that growing numbers of people will benefit from receiving money from their family either when or before they die. This is because the UK is becoming increasingly wealthy. At the moment over 70% of families own their own home and the average value of a home is greater than £100,000. Unfortunately people with learning difficulties do not always achieve their proper inheritance:

Lack of forethought	Some people just have not thought about it or assume that it is okay simply to pass on all their wealth to their non-disabled children in the hope that they will take care of their brother or sister. This is both unfortunate and unfair as the money can be just as important to people with learning difficulties. In fact if your family has a lot of money that you will inherit, they should think about getting advice on how to avoid you having to pay inheritance tax on the money you will receive.
No Trust in Place	As we explored in the first chapter, in order to manage your own money if you have a significant learning difficulty you may need a Trust to be set up to control the money for you. If this is the case you will need to explore setting up a Trust with a lawyer. You can also get help from Mencap or Enable on how to set up a Trust. These days many families are setting up Trusts as a way of reducing the amount of inheritance tax their children will pay. A lawyer who is experienced in this area may also be able to help you design a Trust to suit your situation.
Fear of Benefit Traps	Parents and others also fear that giving money to their son or daughter might lead to them losing state benefits. However, if the Trust is set up in the right way it is possible to get round this problem (you can get advice from Mencap on this matter).

8 Receiving benefits

Most people with learning difficulties do receive benefit payments from the government to help them with some of the everyday costs in life. As benefits are always changing and the rules of entitlement can be quite complicated, it is always worth getting the advice of an independent benefits expert to check you are getting the best deal possible.

In the following table I have set down most of the benefits that people were entitled to in 2005/06 (see Figure 20). But this list is just to help you quickly see some of the possible kinds of benefit. ***Do not rely on this list to help you budget without having taken proper advice; benefits change every year and this information will already be out of date – it is just to give you an idea of what you might get.***

Benefit	What is it for	Weekly amount (2005/06)
Income Support - Personal Allowance (Aged 25 and over)	To help you pay basic living costs if you don't earn enough money	£56.20
Disability Premium (DP) - for a single person	Extra help for ordinary living costs	£23.95
Severe Disability Premium (SDP) - for a single person	Extra help for ordinary living costs if you have a severe disability	£45.50
Disability Living Allowance - Care Component (DLA-C)	To help you pay for help with your disability	£16.05 - £60.60
Disability Living Allowance - Mobility Component (DLA-M)	To help you pay for getting around	£16.05-£42.30
Housing Benefit (HB)	To help you pay your rent	Less than or equal to the actual rent you pay
Mortgage Interest Relief (MIR)	To help you pay a mortgage	Varies with the interest rates

Figure 20 An example of benefits in 2005/06

This table does not even to begin to do justice to the complexity of your entitlement to benefits. Benefits change for all sorts of reasons, for example:

- If you are a young adult or a pensioner.
- If you are married or living as a couple.
- If you have children.
- If you recently lost your job.
- If you have any savings.
- If you need more or less support.

In fact most benefits are given on the basis that the government will only give you the minimum help possible. So as soon as you are able to do without a benefit then you lose your right to claim that benefit. This is called 'means-testing' - giving people money in proportion to their means ('how well off they are'). The effect of this policy is quite important although it is rather unfortunate for anybody who does need benefits. Means-testing means that you may have your benefits reduced:

- If you earn too much.
- If you save too much.
- If you get married or live with someone.
- If you get more independent.

This means benefits create what is called a 'poverty trap'. For as soon as you start to earn, save, build a family or become more independent you can lose out. Sometimes it can feel that it isn't worth doing all these important things.

In practice the most important thing is to get expert advice on your benefits. There are benefit experts up and down the UK, some work for Social Services and some work for charities. The other important thing to remember is that although the benefit system is complicated and that it can create problems for anybody on benefits, the rules are generally more favourable to disabled people than to non-disabled people.

9 Getting individualised funding

Another way of getting money is to get control of the money that is used to pay for the support and help you need as a disabled person. In its most general form this money is called 'individualised funding' and more and more disabled people are beginning to take control of this individualised funding and pay for their own support services.

There are three main ways of getting hold of individualised funding, although they are often combined:

Independent Living Fund (ILF)   The Independent Living Fund is a body that has been set up nationally for the UK to give some disabled people some individualised funding to control, so that they can purchase their own support. The rules for getting ILF are quite complex and you will need to be getting money or services from your local council and receiving the Disability Living Allowance (high care component). If you think you might be entitled, you should work in partnership with your social worker or an expert within your Social Services department to make your claim.

Direct Payments   In 1996 the government passed a law that said that Local Authorities could give people money instead of services if they need help. Since then there has been increasing pressure placed on Local Authorities to make this option available to all disabled people. Again the rules are sometimes complicated (and can vary between different Local Authorities), but in general more and more effort has been made to increase the number of people who can benefit from this measure.

Supporting People Funds   Another source of funding for people with learning difficulties is money that has been provided to help people get support to look after their own tenancies. This money has recently been reorganised and it pays for what is called housing related support, but not what is called personal care. You will need to get up-to-date local advice on how this is being used in your local area.

10 The problem of entitlement

Some disabled people can find it difficult to get money for support. For example, you might be told that you are not disabled enough, that there isn't enough money to fund support, that no place is available or you are not a priority case. This is unacceptable.

Without a doubt you have the right to receive an assessment of your needs. Moreover, once your needs have been assessed the Local Authority and other public agencies must be fair and reasonable about arranging to make sure your needs are met. The Local Authority must also consider all the individual circumstances of your case in reaching their decision. If they do not they could be challenged in court for refusing to fund your support.

It would help if the law was changed not just to give Local Authorities and other agencies responsibilities, but also to make it clear that disabled people have the right to receive support when it is needed for them to lead their own lives.

There are several ways of putting pressure on your Local Authority if you really need to. Ultimately you can pursue the matter through the courts but you may also consider some of the steps I've set out below (see Figure 21). But it is important to note that if you do take these steps, then there can be negative consequences and so you must be careful about how you go about trying to get your needs met.

How you can get help	The unintended consequences
Complain: By creating enough pressure within the Local Authority you may get the help you need.	You have a right to complain and have your complaint heard. But there may be a risk of a breakdown in communication with the Local Authority, leading to confusion and mistrust.
Wait until things reach crisis point: If your present situation becomes utterly intolerable then this will give your case more urgency.	But this can lead to a rapid and inappropriate service instead of a carefully thought-out plan of what you want to do.
Put more emphasis on your needs: If you appear to have very high needs then this can help improve your chances of getting help.	But this can lead to you being over-supported; this could stifle your self-development.
Disguise your Natural Support: If you appear not to have anybody willing or able to offer you help, then you will be seen as more needy.	But this can encourage the creation of services that isolate you from your existing family and friends.

Figure 21 The risks of trying to get your needs met

If you want to get support but you want to avoid any of these negative consequences, I would recommend you take the following steps:

- Describe what has happened so far in your life and what will happen if you don't get support. In other words let the Local Authority know that there could be a crisis if they don't help, but don't make a crisis happen.

- Ask for funding that you or someone you trust can control, but try to make sure that what you ask for is fair and reasonable compared to what other people get. If you can even show that this is a 'good deal' for the Local Authority, then they are more likely to provide the necessary funding.

- Develop your own Support Plan describing what support you want and how you want it delivered. Build in any Natural Support from family or friends that you all genuinely want.

- If at first you do not get the response you want, follow the local complaints procedure. If you complain in a careful and measured way, that will enable the manager who is lower down in the system to respond and you will be more likely to maintain a good relationship. If you have to take your complaint further, always try to be calm and courteous about it, and ask for help in putting your case. An advocate could help you do this, or some Local Authorities have complaints staff who will assist you in putting your complaint forward.

But remember you do not have to accept constant delays. The Local Authority should tell you when it will reply to your complaint. If you are not told then you should make sure that you let them know when you expect to hear from them. If they do not stick to the promised timescales then make sure you also complain about their late response.

One Local Authority that has taken a strong stance in making Direct Payments more available and trying to resolve the problem of entitlements is North Lanarkshire Council in Scotland. It has tried to develop policies that mean anybody who could benefit from having more control of their own support services is eligible for what it calls 'Self-Directed Services'. Its policy is given below (see Figure 22).

Eligibility for Self-Directed Services

In North Lanarkshire the following criteria must be met if someone is entitled to use Self-Directed Services:

1 The individual must be assessed as requiring Community Care Services.

2 The individual wants to use Self-Directed Services. It is important to note that North Lanarkshire Council can judge that someone wants Self-Directed Services when it is clear from their behaviour or other modes of expression that they want to achieve things that are best achieved by using Self-Directed Services. Individuals do *not* need to be able to express their willingness directly or in verbal speech.

3 The individual or, if required, some other person who is prepared to act on the individual's behalf as their Agent, will be required to enter into a formal agreement with North Lanarkshire Council on how the funding allocation will be managed.

4 There must be no significant risk that can only be reduced by North Lanarkshire Council keeping control of the Community Care Service.

5 The individual must not be intending to live in institutional care, other than for respite purposes.

Figure 22 North Lanarkshire Council's Eligibility Policy

Once a person's needs have been assessed and agreed, the Local Authority will try to give an indication of a financial figure that it thinks will be fair and reasonable and which will enable the person to fund the necessary support. The figure would be based on what it would take to support someone with similar needs. Once this figure is available, it enables the individual and the family to develop a realistic plan that fits their own situation.

If national policy can move in this direction it will bring about a revolution in the way disabled people are served. Instead of being people who must wait in line to get the services they are given, disabled people are being given the opportunity to take control and responsibility for the support they need to run their own lives. It is still early days but if you or someone you trust wants to learn more about what can happen for you, then you should approach your local Social Services or Social Work Department. This policy will present new opportunities and new challenges to disabled people and their families and it is to be welcomed strongly.

How to spend your money

Getting hold of your money is one thing. But making good use of it is something else all together. In the following section I want to describe some of the things you will need to spend money on and suggest some simple ways you can make the best use of your finances – wherever they come from.

1 Money for Living

In everyday life there are a set of costs you can plan for that are quite predictable and with a little care you should be able to make sure you can pay for all these costs.

Housing
You need to make sure you can pay your rent or mortgage. These are both such important things that it is best if you can handle the money in a way that there is no temptation for you to spend it. For instance, you can arrange for your Housing Benefit to be paid directly to your landlord; or your Mortgage Interest Relief can be paid directly to the mortgage provider.

Utilities
Utilities are the bills like electricity, gas and even your phone and TV licence. Like your housing costs these are very important and you do not want to end up in a situation where you cannot pay for them. If you think you might end up running up bigger bills than you really have the money for, think about ways to make sure you don't. For instance:

- You could use tokens to 'pay as you go'. This means that you will not create big bills for yourself that you were not expecting.

- You can put money aside in advance. This means you get into the habit of regularly putting money aside and ideally you always put a little bit more than you need. So you are always covered and then you can treat yourself with the money you save when the bill comes around and is less than what you've put aside. In fact some utilities let you do this by buying special stamps that go towards the cost of your bill.

Whatever system you decide to use, do not start ignoring bills. If you really get yourself in trouble and spend more than you can afford then talk to the utility provider, explain your situation. As they don't really want to cut off a customer they will normally help you make the payments over time.

Food

We all need to eat and eating can be one of the great pleasures of life. It is also an area where it can become quite easy to spend more than you can afford. It's a good idea to know how much you are going to spend each week on food. Cooking food yourself or getting supporters to cook meals for you is much cheaper than buying food out or getting a take-away.

Transport

You will need to put money aside for transport, whether you travel by bus, train or car.

Savings

As well as all the regular things, it is important to put aside any money for bigger things and emergencies. So as well as your regular payments you need to think about all the other things you might need money for:

- Furniture.
- Equipment, e.g. a television or computer.
- Holidays.
- Presents.
- Emergencies.

A good idea is to save by putting a bit of your regular money aside into a special pot that you do not normally touch.

A good book on managing your money is *Money for Life* by Alvin Hall. This book gives more tips on staying in good financial shape, not spending too much and planning for the future.

If possible draw up a budget that counts up everything you've got coming in and everything going out. I have provided a real example of a budget below (see Figure 23).

A Real Budget

This is an example of a real budget. It was the budget for two sisters who lived together. One of them had a learning difficulty and the other helped her and also employed a neighbour to provide additional support.

Income	Monthly	Yearly
Benefits for sister with disability (IS, DLA & SDA)	£433.00	£5,196.00
Benefits for other sister (IS)	£263.90	£3,166.80
DSS Mortgage Payment	£250.00	£3,000.00
Sister's Earnings	£58.50	£702.00
Individual Service Fund	£1,944.00	£23,328.00
Mobility Allowance	£129.00	£1,548.00
TOTAL	**£3,078.40**	**£36,940.80**

Expenditure	Monthly	Yearly
Mortgage Interest	£240.00	£2,880.00
Gas	£50.00	£600.00
Electricity	£47.20	£566.40
Council Tax	£10.00	£120.00
Food	£200.00	£2,400.00
Household goods	£40.00	£480.00
Telephone	£32.00	£384.00
TV	£8.00	£96.00
Clothing & linen	£100.00	£1,200.00
Furniture	£50.00	£600.00
Electrical goods	£40.00	£480.00
Car leasing	£129.00	£1,548.00
Petrol	£40.00	£480.00
Entertainment	£40.00	£480.00
Support Service	£2000.00	£24,000.00
Emergencies and savings	£50.00	£600.00
TOTAL	**£3,076.20**	**£36,914.40**

Figure 23 An example of a real budget

2 Money for Support

If you are going to take responsibility for planning your own service, then there are a number of things you need to do to work out how much your service will cost and to make sure you have covered some costs that you might not have thought of at first. There are a number of people who will give more detailed advice about this, including Centres for Independent Living. There is also a detailed manual on employing your own supporters by Martin Yates which is called *When is Support Most Effective? When It's Not Visible.*

In the following section I will set out the main things you need to think about. But the most important thing I would say is that if this all seems too forbidding, don't be put off too quickly. Go and talk to some of the people who are already doing this. Employing staff and purchasing services is a very effective way of staying in control of your own life.

Salary

One of the most important decisions you must make is to decide how much to offer someone to come and work for you. Partially you will need to look at the salaries other people are paying but there are other factors to think about too:

- Will it be fun and rewarding to work for you?

- Will they form a strong relationship with you?

- Will there be any other perks or benefits to working with you?

- What hours will you be asking people to work and how flexible will they need to be?

There is a rather awful phrase that people use: "If you pay peanuts you get monkeys." But this is not only rude it is also untrue. You cannot measure someone by the salary they earn or want, you simply have to try and work out what seems both fair and reasonable in your situation.

Of course if you are negotiating to get funding for your supporters, then it makes sense to get the best deal you can so that you can pay people as much as you can reasonably afford. But there is no strong relationship between how much you pay and the quality of the support you receive. This is probably because the main reason someone chooses to work with you, after they have attained a certain level of pay, is for the pleasure and satisfaction they get from spending time with you. If they are not happy to work with you then paying them more is unlikely to make much difference; if they are happy to work with you then money is not the only thing that is keeping them in the job.

National Insurance	As well as the salary you pay somebody you will have to pay the government a tax for the pleasure of being an employer. This tax is called National Insurance. The rate of this tax changes every year. You will need to make sure that if a Local Authority is giving you money, that they change this money when the government changes the National Insurance rates.
Pension	It is very important that you encourage anybody working for you to have a pension. (In fact you may want to do this yourself and set up your own pension.) Employers are expected to make a contribution to any pension that the individual takes out.
Holidays	People will also need paid holidays. You will need to let them take holidays and have arrangements so you can pay other people to support you if necessary while they are away. This means you might need extra money in your budget to cover these costs.
Sickness and maternity leave	A more difficult thing to plan for is what to do if people go sick or take maternity leave. People have the right to be paid by their employer for the first weeks of sickness and maternity leave and so it is worth getting advice on how much you should put in your budget to cover these possibilities.
Redundancy	If you make people redundant who have been working for you for a long time, then you may also need to pay redundancy money to them. Again it is worth getting advice about this when you make up your budget.
Services	As well as paying people directly (employing people) you can buy services from people or organisations. For instance you might pay for:

- Support from a Support Organisation.

- Payroll services from a Finance Organisation.

- Therapy from a specialist Therapist.

- The services of a self-employed person.

The downside of paying for services is that they can be more expensive than doing it for yourself. But the good side is that they take responsibility for organising things like National Insurance, pensions, etc. and if you don't get the service you want you can just stop paying for it.

Contingencies	It is also best to put aside money in your budget for 'contingencies', which is just a fancy word for unexpected things that happen. Sometimes Local Authorities are

uncomfortable with allowing payments made for contingencies. But this is very important and if they cannot be persuaded, try to find another part of the budget where you can put some 'safety money'.

Equipment, capital or cars

Another important thing to explore is whether there is any advantage in spending money on a thing: a car, a piece of equipment or a change to your house. Often this can be a much better use of your money. However, if a Local Authority or Health Authority is unwilling to put forward all the money in one year, it may be possible to borrow the money to buy the thing and pay it back over a few years out of your budget.

Staff expenses

Another very important thing to think about is how you are going to pay any necessary membership fees, entrance fees or other costs that might be involved in going about living your life. It is usually best to set aside some money so that you can also pay for your staff when you want them to come too.

To give you an idea of how much different services cost, I have put some examples in the table below (see Figure 24). These are all real examples of the different ways of supporting people who need help 24 hours a day and they are all based on real services. The different costs reflect different ways of being supported. Obviously these budgets would change depending upon the basic salary you would use, but I have included not just the basic salary costs but also management support, administration, expenses, training and back-up or contingency costs. I hope this is useful as a starting point for thinking about what you might need, but clearly you need to work this out in detail.

Model of support	Possible Total Cost
24-hour come-in support: This service offers 24 hours of support seven days per week. Staff are paid sleep-over payments for staying over at the home of the individual.	£62,650
Come-in support plus supportive flatmates: This service offers 24-hour support, but some night-time and evening support is provided by supportive flatmates.	£51,320
Live-in plus come-in support: This service offers 24 hours of support but combines paid live-in and come-in support.	£43,700
Family plus come-in support: This service provides 24-hour support by combining unpaid family support with paid support from workers employed by the family.	£29,260

Figure 24 Costs of 24-hour Support Services

3 Being smart with your money

As well as drawing up a sensible and well-planned budget there are also some other tricks to managing your money well.

Set cash limits A good way of controlling what you or other people spend is to set cash limits. This means setting aside the money as cash (notes and coins) instead of using cheques or cards. This means there is no danger of overspending and the money left over can always be put towards something fun.

For example one woman and her support team put aside the money they saved from the weekly travel allowance. By the end of the year they had saved enough money for a big family party.

Don't pay tax on service funding Even if you receive funding for your support service you should not pay income tax on that money. It is not given to you as an income and the Inland Revenue does not expect you to treat it as income, so you do not have to pay tax on it.

Monitor it Find a way of regularly checking how much money you have and how much you've saved. You should keep records and receipts of the money you spend if possible so that you can check if you are being realistic about what your lifestyle costs.

Build in incentives Make sure that you and the people who support you have positive incentives to control your money. For example, Dan used to be very careful about not spending too much on his bills. He knew that if he kept the cost of his bills below the money he had set aside for them then he could use the difference to buy tickets to see Tottenham Hotspurs.

Avoid debt One of the most important things to remember is not to borrow money unless it is absolutely necessary and you have a good plan of how to get out of debt. Debt is very dangerous because borrowing money is very expensive and if you even just begin to fail to pay back what you owe, it can become even more expensive.

I hope this chapter has not been too dry and dusty. After talking about grand themes like 'self-determination' and Person Centred Planning, to talk about money can seem grubby and boring. But money is not boring and understanding how to get and use money is one of the keys to citizenship in the modern world. Without money you must rely totally on the kindness of others. But you cannot feel like a citizen, as an equal, if you are totally dependent on others and with no control over your own destiny. Having money is a necessary part of having control over your life in the modern world. For this reason money is the third key to citizenship.

Organisations that can help with advice and support about benefits or Direct Payments

Andrew Holman, tel: 0870 740 4887, email: andrew@communityliving.org.uk

Child Poverty Action Group, 94 White Lion Street, London N1 9PF,
tel: 0207 837 7979, website: www.cpag.org.uk

Department for Work and Pensions (DWP), Correspondence Unit, Room 540,
The Adelphi, 1-11 John Adam Street, London WC2N 6HT, tel: 0207 712 2171,
website: www.dwp.gov.uk

Direct Payments Scotland, Update, 27 Beaverhall Road, Edinburgh EH7 4JE,
0131 558 5200, email: info@dpscoltand.org.uk

Disability Alliance, Universal House, 88-94 Wentworth Street, London E1 7SA,
tel: 0207 247 8776, website: www.disabilityalliance.org

National Centre for Independent Living, 250 Kennington Lane, London SE11
5RD, tel: 0207 587 1663, email: ncil@ncil.org.uk

Values Into Action, Oxford House, Derbyshire Street, London E2 6HG,
tel: 0207 729 5436, website: www.viauk.org

Useful reading

Bolles, R.N., *What Color is Your Parachute?,* Ten Speed Press, 2003

Department of Work and Pensions, *Helping Sick and Disabled people Get Jobs*,
DWP 2003

Hall, A., *Money for Life,* Hodder & Stoughton, 2000

Henderson, E. & Bewley, C., *Too Little, Too Slowly,* Values Into Action Discussion
Paper, 2000

Yates, M., *When is Support Most Effective? – When It's Not Visible,*
Yates's Press, 1999

KEY FOUR: HOME

The fourth key to citizenship is to have a home. Having a home is a fundamental human right. It roots us in a community and the possession of a home helps other citizens to see us as a genuine part of the community. If we have a home, we belong, we are staying and other people have to recognise our presence. We are somebody who has a stake in the community; we will be affected if things go wrong; we must take some responsibility for the world we share with others. Of course this is not the only reason we value having a home. There are many practical advantages to having a home:

1 A place of safety

A home can give you shelter. It is a place where you should feel safe and secure. It is for this reason that the most important thing about any home is not where it is but who lives with you. For if you feel secure and confident about the people you live with, then you will feel safe in your own home. However, if you feel vulnerable in your home, then your home will no longer feel safe.

Unfortunately the Registered Care Homes or what are sometimes called 'homes' where people are 'put' are often very unsafe. Residents in one of these kinds of home have no real choice about who does or does not live with them. So you cannot be sure that you won't have to share your home with someone you don't get on with or even with someone who might abuse you.

2 A place you control

A home is a place that you control. It looks the way you want it to look, it is filled with your property and you determine how you want to live within your home. In a sense the home gives us what community life can never give us, a sense of control over the passing minutes and hours. If we work or play with others then we will have to compromise with them and often we just have to fit in with them. But in our home we can 'do our own thing', we can relax, we can be ourselves. These are precious qualities.

Again the residential homes on offer to people with learning difficulties really struggle to provide the people who live in them any real control over their own homes. This is not just because people can find it very difficult to live together. The main reason that a residential home is not a place you can control is that the home is really a work place for the staff who support you. As their work place it is very easy for the rotas, the schedules and the organisational policies to dominate. These things leave very little room for you to just be, to relax and to feel in control.

When families who have children with disabilities receive support in their own home, that they cannot control, they are almost always left frustrated. The family feels powerless as forces outside their own control invade their routines, rituals and spaces. But if that is the experience of most families why would it be any different for adults with disabilities, living in their own home? We value having our space and we want to control who comes into that space and what they do when they are in it.

3 A private place

Home is essentially a private place. Couples 'set up home' together and it is within the home that we have sex lives and where our children are brought up. There is an appropriate privacy to our own homes. This privacy might be thought of as a retreat, an escape from the gaze of others, for reasons of modesty or just as a place where there is no need to perform.

But again such privacy is hard to maintain within a care home. First there are the people you live with, from whom you may need to protect yourself. Second there are the staff, whom you do not choose and may be unable to control or influence. Third there is your own vulnerability and lack of privacy. If you live in a care home you are examined in every detail; there is nowhere to hide. Other people know about your sex life, your toilet habits, your eating habits, your sleeping habits and they often believe that they are entitled to change those habits to make them easier on themselves, more normal or less damaging to other residents. I am not arguing that all such interventions are wrong; but imagine how it feels to have nothing that is genuinely private, no place to go that is just your own.

4 A base for your life

The fourth quality of a good home is that it is the right base for the life you want to lead. This is fundamentally a matter of the home's location. Each of us has a lifestyle that is most appropriate for us. This is made up of our work, time with our family and friends, what we do for fun and for our own development. All these things are made easier or more difficult by the location of our home.

When people with learning difficulties are put in a 'home' then location is only thought about in the most limited way. Usually the Local Authority will want to place you in a local service, close to the day centre, the specialist health service and the social work service that it controls or can influence. However, sometimes the opposite principle applies. When the Local Authority feels that the individual is someone it cannot successfully support, then it is quite typical to see the individual moved to a specialist hospital or care home many miles from the Local Authority. This person will be considered too challenging for local services and they must therefore be put wholly in the hands of some specialist service.

In ordinary life the decision about where to live is a complex decision where we have to balance consideration of many factors:

- Where can we afford to live?

- Do we want to live close to particular friends or family?

- Where will be convenient for work?

- What kind of community or environment will suit our lifestyle?

There is no scientific method for deciding the right location for our home but by thinking about these kinds of factors we can usually narrow down our choice to a very limited set of possible locations. These locations are the places that we identify as good bases for our life.

5 An asset

For many people in the UK a home is also an asset. It may have been inherited from parents or it may have been partially paid for from the sale of a parent's home. Even for people who rent their homes from Local Authorities or from social landlords, it is often possible that they will be able to pass on their homes to their children when they die.

The importance of the home as an asset is not limited to the obvious advantages that money brings. Passing on a home often serves to provide an important link between the generations, reinforcing the links between grandparents, parents and children and the critical family component of our identity.

Some people with learning difficulties have parents who plan ahead and ensure that they are able by some means or other to obtain a stake in the home and other family assets. However, some people lose this opportunity. This can happen because families are unaware that they can pass on assets using Trusts or other legal mechanisms. Sometimes families themselves rely on services so much that they think the individual has no need of the assets, for the Local Authority will provide everything they need. Sometimes people in public sector housing lose their tenancies because the Local Authority fails to organise support for the person to stay in their family home. This failure to receive anything from the previous generation is a denial of the individual's place in the family story.

Why Supported Living is important

Homes are important to all of us, but people with learning difficulties have generally been denied the opportunity to have a home. That is, unless they and their family are simply prepared to carry on living together (a state which is not in itself bad but which can create a certain tension between parent and adult son or daughter).

Instead of a home, people have been 'offered' either a bed within a hospital or a 'place' within a 'home'. A 'home' that is not a home. If you go into hospital then you become a 'patient', a word that means you are someone who is being 'done to', someone who is passive. If you move into a care home then you become a 'resident', which means that you 'stay there', but this does not imply you have any control or ownership over where you live.

In the UK there has been a slow process of change that has started to offer people better alternatives. Since the 1960s the number of people with learning difficulties living in hospital has been reducing. In 1968 there were 65,000 people living in hospital in England alone. In 2000 there were 10,000 people living in residential services managed by the NHS (a mixture of hospital services and NHS residential homes). This same process has seen a significant increase in the number of people with learning difficulties living in care homes, with 53,400 people living in residential care homes. However, since the early 1990s, there have also been a small but growing number of people supported to live in their own homes. The simple idea that people with learning difficulties should be able to have their own homes has acquired a name, Supported Living.

The inhumane practice of shutting people away in hospitals and of putting people in care homes has left its mark. Even when people know that this is wrong, they still tend to think that we just need to find a new model of service for people with learning difficulties. In a slightly more sophisticated form, this question becomes 'What is the right *range* of service models?' This way of thinking about people with learning difficulties treats them as objects, to be slotted into the right shape service slots. It does not treat people as fellow citizens who have the right to make their own decisions and plans in their own way.

Supported Living is not about offering an alternative 'model' to residential care homes or hospitals. Instead it is the claim that people are entitled, as citizens, to live in their own homes. This is not because it is the best 'treatment for people with learning difficulties' - it is a fundamental human right. People who promote Supported Living are therefore simply drawing attention to the fact that people have the right to a real home, not a home just in name, but a genuine home. And for a home to be real you should:

- Be able to choose who you live with.
- Be able to control who comes in and out of your home, including the people who support you.
- Be able to live as you wish in your home.
- Be able to choose where you live.
- Have tenancy rights or own your own home.

In my experience, applying these principles seems to lead to many more people living either on their own or with a small number of friends, family or live-in supporters that they have chosen. Unsurprisingly these choices are similar to the choices that other people in the community make.

What are your housing options?

There are lots of things to consider if you are thinking about setting up home. You need to think about:

- Where you want to live?
- What kind of house you want or need to live in?
- What kind of control you want over your housing?
- What kind of responsibility you want for your housing?
- Who you should live with, if anybody?

The following list of do's and don'ts was drawn up to help people avoid the trap of assuming that they had to live in the same way that people with learning difficulties have had to live in the past (see Figure 25). This is only a guide to help you think through what is right for you.

Do	Don't
Do think about whether you want to live with other people: Would you benefit financially or socially from sharing your home with others?	**Don't** assume all disabled people want to live together. Sometimes it is even important to some people that they don't live with another disabled person.
Do choose who you live with: If you do want to live with other people, how are you going to be involved in selecting your flatmates?	**Don't** assume people won't want to live with someone with a learning difficulty: Have you got a friend, boyfriend or girlfriend you would like to share your house with? Remember you are allowed to make decisions that you might come to regret - as long as you are able to separate and move on.
Do think about what kind of house would be suitable: How many rooms are necessary? Will you have many visitors or guests? Will the house need to be accessible for someone in a wheelchair?	**Don't** assume adaptations can't be made to properties: Would your existing home form a good base? Could you buy it or take it over from your parents?
Do choose where you want to live: Is there a neighbourhood you already like and are familiar with? How will you be involved in house-hunting?	**Don't** assume you must live close to other disabled people or existing services: Do you want to link up with any particular support organisation?
Do think about your financial situation: Is it important that you build up any capital in the form of property or that you spend cash that would otherwise affect your benefits?	**Don't** assume that there is no value in owning property: Home ownership would give you additional opportunities in the future and is a relatively safe way of receiving assets from another family member.
Do think about flexibility: How likely is it that this will be a long-term home or do you expect to move again quite soon?	**Don't** assume people will always want to live in the same place forever: How do you see your life evolving in the years to come?
Do look at the neighbourhood: What kinds of things will you be doing with your life? Who or what will you be visiting regularly? Are there likely to be any problems with neighbours?	**Don't** assume there's one kind of right environment for disabled people: Some people like quiet areas, some people like the bustle of the town. What would be right for you?

Figure 25 Housing issues to think about

Unfortunately getting hold of housing for anyone in the UK is not always easy, particularly as many people with learning difficulties are unemployed and depend upon the benefits system. However, although there are difficulties, there are many ways of overcoming those difficulties. The basic forms of housing from which you can choose are set out in the table below (see Figure 26):

Housing Choices	Pros	Cons
Council Housing	Affordable Housing Benefit Secure tenancy Right to buy Maintenance costs low	Limited choice and control over locations or house types Long waiting lists for more desirable areas or properties Can be difficult to move
Housing Association	Affordable Housing Benefit Secure tenancy More likely to be 'barrier free' May specialise in housing for people with particular needs Maintenance costs low	Limited locations Limited choice Limited house types Long waiting lists for more desirable areas Can be difficult to move May have a restrictive allocation policy
Private rent	Choice Some Housing Benefit Can be quick Flexible, easy to move	Not secure Can be expensive Tenancy terms generally limit control
Owning/buying	Choice Control Financial asset Income Support Mortgage Interest (ISMI)	Initial costs - deposit, fees Maintenance costs
Shared ownership	Financial asset Housing Benefit (if LA/HA)	Limited choice Maintenance costs Less control than outright ownership
Family buying to let	Choice Control Financial asset Housing Benefit	Initial capital outlay or capital tied up Maintenance costs More limited sense of independence
Trust owning and/or letting	Choice Control Financial asset Housing Benefit if applicable Can be very secure	Initial capital outlay or capital tied up Maintenance costs More limited sense of independence Management dependent on quality of Trustees

Figure 26 Different forms of housing

The various advantages and disadvantages of these forms of housing need to be reviewed in the light of your needs and desires and the opportunities or difficulties within the local area. I will go on to describe in more detail four of the main ways you can get a home:

- Renting from the public-voluntary sector.

- Renting in the private market.

- Buying your own home.

- Staying in your family home.

The proportion of housing rented by the public, voluntary and private sectors along with the proportion of homeowners varies from locality to locality. Clearly if you are in an area where say, home ownership dominates, the availability of rented housing may be very low.

What is critical is that you get good advice about your housing options. There will rarely be any organisation that can offer perfect advice. Most organisations will have their own narrow understanding of what is possible and will suffer from a limited sense of what is possible for people with learning difficulties. However you could talk to:

- Local housing officers of the Local Authority and any local Housing Associations.

- Local representatives of the national housing organisations: Communities Scotland, Housing Corporation.

- Advocacy or advice organisations like the Disabled Persons Housing Service, Housing Options or Ownership Options in Scotland.

- Estate agents and letting agents.

Possibly the best way of finding out how to do it locally is to ask somebody who has already done it. However, this relies on someone else breaking new ground. Why should it not be you who does it in a way that nobody has done before? Peter's story (see Figure 27) gives you an example of a family who did things in their own way even when they knew nobody who had ever gone down that path before.

How to rent from the public-voluntary sector

Most people with learning difficulties who have their own home have found that home by renting it either from a Local Authority (council housing) or from the voluntary sector (Housing Association or housing co-op). Although there are differences between Local Authority and voluntary sector housing, both forms are so inter-linked that it is best to consider them together.

Both Local Authorities and voluntary sector organisations stress that the purpose of their offering housing is to ensure that people in greater need can get access to housing. However, this does not always mean that people with learning difficulties will be treated as a priority.

Local Authority policies vary and some Local Authorities operate in a way that makes it very effective at identifying possible housing for people who have been assessed as requiring community care services. The first step therefore will almost always be getting a community care assessment that will include an assessment of housing need. It is important at this point to have already done some work on what you think is best for you. You should try to develop your case by considering:

- Why you need new housing.

- What kind of housing you need as an alternative.

- Where that housing should be.

- How many bedrooms you will need.

You should then try to persuade the social worker (or care manager) who is doing the assessment of your case. They may be very experienced and be able to advise you of how likely it is you can achieve what you want. However, you may also find that they are rather inexperienced and if they are putting you off looking for what you want, it is because they have no experience of achieving it. Always be prepared to ask around and persist in the face of initial reluctance.

Once you have developed your case and come to an agreement with your social worker on what is appropriate, then you need to explore what the system is for prioritising housing. Often housing is made available by a points system. Make sure you know what the system is and make sure that you have identified every possible means by which your points can be maximised.

In general all systems try to give priority to people in worse situations; therefore you should not play down your disability or any problems you are having. You should clearly state what's not working about your present situation and should stress the harm it is doing you and any others involved. Unfortunately being good at coping with difficult circumstances is not treated as a reason to give you high priority - so don't be seen to cope too well.

The other important matter to resolve is whether you need also to try voluntary sector organisations in parallel to the council. While most Local Authorities can refer people on to voluntary sector organisations, it may well also be worth approaching the voluntary sector organisations separately. They will also have waiting lists and some criteria for prioritising people and the same principles apply as above.

Going through these doorways can be tiring and dispiriting. You need to answer lots of questions, persuade and sometimes even badger people. What you can achieve is rarely the best housing available, although sometimes the housing is excellent. Usually the cost of housing is controlled to bring it within the available levels of Housing Benefit, so housing costs are normally not an issue.

Arguably the security of most public and voluntary sector housing far exceeds what is available in the private sector, but that is rather double-edged. Once you are housed you may have to wait many years before you can move again and if you lose your tenancy in the public sector it can be doubly difficult to get access to public-sector housing again. However, people heavily involved in the provision of public-sector housing tend to emphasise its benefits and you can sometimes find some people too eager to close down the other ways of getting a house for what seem to be political reasons. But if either the route to public-sector housing looks too difficult or the final housing options are not attractive enough, then you should seriously consider one of the other two routes to accessing a new home: either renting or buying a house in the private sector.

How to rent in the private market

The private rented market is not very developed in the United Kingdom; however, there will almost certainly be a range of properties to rent in any area. Houses are usually let in one of three ways:

Directly	Usually landlords will advertise their properties themselves in the local newspapers and will deal with you directly about the lease and any practical matters to do with the property.
Via Letting Agencies	Sometimes landlords strike deals with letting agencies or estate agencies that will take on the administration of advertising and dealing with the lease. The agency may or may not also take on responsibility for repairs instead of the landlord. The agency takes a cut of the money received but the landlord still bears most of the risk.
Via Housing Agencies	Sometimes private landlords will sign leases with third parties like Housing Associations, voluntary organisations or universities in order that they can pass on the full responsibility of letting the property to the final tenants. In this case the landlord is getting a smaller return but is letting the third party take the risk that they will not find any tenants.

Obviously to identify potential properties you will then need to find out which local newspapers are used to advertise properties for rent or by using the Internet where many properties are now advertised. In addition you will need to go through the Yellow Pages and identify any letting agencies.

The primary barrier for renting in the private sector will be price, as some properties will be rented at prices that exceed what the Housing Benefit system will pay. However, it is important that you get good local advice from a welfare rights person. The Housing Benefit system is controlled by a complex set of rules, which are interpreted differently in different localities. Often people are prepared to be more flexible in the case of disabled people so it is important to ensure that you do not take the first piece of information for granted. For instance, if you need an extra room for a live-in supporter and you have a disability then Housing Benefit will cover the higher cost. However, front-line officials do not always know the detailed rules that apply to disabled people.

The second barrier may be prejudice. However, this is frequently double-edged. For although some people may not want to have anything to do with someone with a learning difficulty just as many people are likely to be more than willing to make a special effort to work out what it will take for someone to rent their property. What you need to think about is the impression you make:

- Be serious about what you are trying to do - you want to rent a property and you are not looking for any special favours on the rent etc. If the individual has no experience of renting to people on benefits explain to them how much security that will give them as a landlord.

- Show that you understand you will have responsibilities, not just to pay the rent but to take care of the property and be a good neighbour. Talk about yourself, what you are hoping to do in your new home, exhibit your positive qualities and the qualities that other neighbours will appreciate.

- Let people know that you have a clear and guaranteed support system to help you fulfil your obligations. Sometimes your supporters may even be willing to offer to put their commitment to you in writing to the landlord in what is called a 'management agreement'.

Renting in the private sector is a much more personal business. There is none of the political persuasion needed to get through the public-sector doorways. Instead you are seeking to strike a good deal with a private individual and that individual primarily wants to know that the rent will be paid and that there won't be lots of additional problems created by trouble from neighbours or damage to the property. Things can go wrong and you are unlikely to achieve enormous security of tenure and you may be given only a few months' notice before you have to quit. But when it works well the landlord can be a powerful ally and even a friend, someone with a real understanding of your situation who will discuss problems with you directly and with no bureaucracy.

How to buy your own home

Unfortunately most people with learning difficulties rely on state benefits for their living. Frequently this has led people to suppose that this means that there is no possibility that they can buy their own homes. However, the rules of state benefits do allow for the possibility of home ownership, in particular it is possible that the DSS will pay mortgage interest payments when a move to home ownership is required in order to better meet someone's needs.

In fact there are increasing numbers of people with learning difficulties taking the option of shared or full home ownership. In particular two brokerage agencies Ownership Options in Scotland and Housing Options have been offering advice on how to do home ownership for some time now. In Scotland alone nearly 50 people have been supported to buy their own home. Inclusion Glasgow, a support provider, has supported seven people to buy their own homes after leaving a long-stay institution.

There are, however, a number of obstacles to home ownership. Some of these matters are described in more detail in Nigel King's book *Ownership Options* and in *Home Truths* by Vicki Butler and Julia Fitzpatrick. Here I will set out some of these issues and describe how they have been overcome.

1 Identifying who will own the house

If home ownership is being considered the most critical issue to determine is *who* is going to buy the house. Some of the options that have been used include:

Individual acts totally on their own behalf	This is the most immediately obvious model, for it is the model ordinarily used by other adults buying their own homes. However, this model can only be used if the lawyer acting on your behalf is satisfied that you can understand what they are doing. This is a question of judgement, but clearly there are going to be many people for whom this means that this model will not be possible.
Individuals using a power of attorney	You can also ask another person to act on your behalf. This can be done so that the representative is only given those powers that are necessary to buy a house. However, this depends upon your being able to clearly agree to such an arrangement, and there are going to be some people who cannot provide that level of consent.
Using a representative or Trust	If you cannot consent to a power of attorney then you need a Trust or representative to purchase the house for you. This will involve getting some suitable legal solution from a lawyer.
A family buying it themselves	Although this would not be home ownership by the disabled person it does seem possible for a house purchase to be made by a family member, where the family member is the owner. The family may still be entitled to claim benefits to cover the cost of the interest on the mortgage.
Joint ownership	Another way of owning your home is to bring in another homeowner. This can be done in a number of ways but the three most common are (a) buying it with a Housing Association (this is often called Shared Ownership) (b) buying it with a family member or (c) buying it with a cohabitee (someone you live with). The latter two options are straightforward and simply act so as to reduce the cost of home ownership by giving somebody else a stake in the home. The main issue to consider is the likely durability of the relationship. I will not discuss this in detail but if you are interested in it you will need to explore the possible advantages and disadvantages with both your bank and possible joint owner. Sometimes Housing Associations have developed detailed arrangements for shared ownership, but these will have their own rules and you will need to meet with them to explore whether their arrangements will suit you.

2 Paying for the house

There are two main things to consider when working out how a house is going to be paid for:

Getting a deposit

Deposits are particularly valuable because they can bring the interest rate payable down, sometimes well below the rate remunerated by the DSS. They also provide the bank with more assurance and ease any sense of risk attached to the purchase of the house. The sources for a deposit are various but include:

- Personal assets.
- Family assets.
- Grants from statutory bodies.
- Service funding.
- Grants from the Housing Corporation or Communities Scotland.
- Charitable grants.

There may be other individuals or agencies who want to help the individual purchase their house and who may be prepared to provide funding with suitable terms. For example, in the case of the Smith Family the Health Authority was able pay the service provider who was then able to provide the family with the resources to make the necessary deposit (see Figure 31).

Borrowing money

Banks want to lend money, that's their business; they just need to be reassured that they will get their money back. Once they begin to understand the issues involved they can be valuable allies in promoting home ownership as they can see that home ownership actually provides them with a higher degree of security than is ordinarily possible. It is therefore important to get good advice on the benefits you will be entitled to and then to explore the best way of organising your mortgage. The mortgage market is always changing and so I will offer no advice on the details of how to borrow money. The Financial Services Authority provides information on available mortgage options.

Note that it is important to maximise your personal income. Banks often (although not always) limit what they can lend to you in proportion to your income. If you live on benefits that income may be very low (say £6,000 per year) and so if the bank will lend you only three times your income you may not be able to borrow enough to buy a house. However, you need to look at other income you may have to see whether that could be treated as income. If you receive funding from the Independent Living Fund (which could be up to £20,000 per year) or you receive a Direct Payment then this support funding can be treated as personal income for the purpose of borrowing. In the case of Peter his Individual Service Fund was £60,000 per year. This meant the bank was very willing to lend him the £67,400 he needed to buy his house. The bank simply had to be reassured that this money could in principle be used to support the loan (not that it was intended for that purpose - which it was not). This issue is also becoming less critical for some banks, as they begin to understand the regulations, are now relaxing the rule regarding the income of the individual and will lend on the basis that the DSS will pay the interest.

3 Identifying a lender

Several banks and Building Societies have lent money to people with learning difficulties. In particular, in Scotland The Royal Bank of Scotland and The Dunfermline Building Society have both been very supportive. It is quite likely that banks will quickly develop more confidence in this area if it appears to represent an opportunity for their own development.

4 Paying the interest

There may of course be some people who do not need to rely on benefits to pay for their mortgage, and if so that should be a straightforward financial matter. However, for most people with learning difficulties interest payments will rely on the DSS Income Support regulations.

While the people served by this model are always likely to be entitled to Income Support of various kinds the detail of government policy is always likely to be in flux. It will therefore be necessary to get the support of the best welfare advice you can. However, in general, it seems safe to assume that while the regulations are complex they have also been designed to positively include disabled people, where home ownership offers a genuinely better way of meeting their needs. In order to pursue a benefit claim the following people need to be contacted:

DWP officials   It would also be appropriate to make contact with the relevant personnel within the Department of Work and Pensions (DWP). Given the overall economic efficiency of these arrangements and the fact that a house purchase would only be considered if it did better meet the needs of the individual then it is likely that officers within those organisations will be supportive.

Social Services officials   It will normally make sense to get the full support of the local social work department in any changes that are being made to the individual's support and housing. The Local Authority may even be able to provide financial support, particularly if a third party, possibly even the Trust is involved. The Local Authority might also be able to turn existing or future services into a Direct Payment that will help you borrow more. The Local Authority is also a helpful ally in working with other agencies.

Brokerage services   The two major brokerage services are Ownership Options in Scotland and Housing Options and they will provide expert advice and support.

Expert benefit advice   Local advisers are often very knowledgeable of the local system and eager to support innovative ideas and services. Often they will know of precedents locally and they will know whom to contact within the DSS.

It is also important to remember that if you have not been receiving Income Support for 39 weeks before you try to get help from the DWP you may have to wait for 39 weeks before they will contribute to the mortgage. This is another area where detailed advice is necessary, as the rules are quite complex. It is also important to note that the rate at which the DWP support the interest on a mortgage may vary from that of the real interest. Over the life time of the loan this should not cause any difficulties, but it does mean that it is best if you can put some money aside just in case there are times when you need to pay more than the DWP are paying.

5 Getting a lawyer

One of the most important but potentially most difficult aspects of this work is to identify a lawyer who is competent to do the work involved. As all these arrangements are somewhat different to the norm it is not uncommon to find that lawyers cannot cope. Experience suggests that it is best if:

- You have only one lawyer to act on your behalf and any others who might be involved. This reduces the cost, confusion and game-playing that you can have with too many lawyers.

- You use a lawyer you know you can trust from past experience.

- You get an agreement from the lawyer to work on a fixed fee basis, as there can be a lot of unexpected work, especially if it's the first time they've done something like this.

6 First steps

First steps should include the following:

- Work out if there are real benefits that will arise from owning a home. In particular are there things about the location, size or other factors which make it likely that it is only by buying a property that you will get a suitable home.

- Discuss the idea with people who are important to you and then seek out the best sources of support and advice that you can. In particular you may want to get the support of your social worker and ensure you have some way of accessing some money for a deposit.

- Identify a lender, and seek a decision in principle about how much you should be able to borrow. Start off with your own bank if you have a good relationship with them and if the local staff know nothing about mortgages for disabled people then check out whether the central staff do. Start discussions about the type of mortgage you want.

- Find an expert benefit adviser and talk over your situation and check that they can help you fill in the necessary forms when the time comes. Clarify what your benefits are likely to be when you move into your new home.

- Do a budget for the house purchase and an income and expenditure budget for the household costs. Work out what you need to live on and what you can afford to borrow.

- Start looking for houses. If you are not certain that you will be able to afford to buy the house get the bank to look at how it could finance it and consider how this will leave you financially.

- If the option appears feasible and attractive then it will be worth identifying a lawyer and contacting the DSS and others to begin the process of house purchase.

Although this process may seem off-putting because it is still in its infancy there is no doubt that things are changing and that the idea of home ownership is becoming acceptable and more readily understood. With commitment the idea can be made a reality, and once it is done once it becomes much easier to repeat. Although this won't be much comfort if you are the first person to do it in your area. Overall I suppose, for all its difficulties, my experience of helping people buy homes is that it is much less difficult than it appears and that it can bring great rewards to everybody involved. In a way the difficulties of home ownership are no greater than the difficulties of getting appropriate public-sector housing. But the difficulties are all there to be dealt with; for it is you or your friends, family or allies who need to deal with almost every stage of the process.

The most difficult but necessary thing to achieve is a positive attitude. Banks want to lend money, lawyers want to do deals, house sellers want to sell their homes; the DSS even wants to give you an entitlement (well almost). If you are competing with other people it is usually only a very small number of other people. But you need to stay positive. If the bank, the seller, the lawyer thinks that you don't believe it is going to happen then they will lose faith too. You need to talk a good game and reassure them that others have already done this, that it will work and that it is important to you to make it work.

It is also important to use your existing contacts. Explore using your bank or your family's bank. Try using personal networks to identify a good lawyer. Look for the house yourself or get your family to help. In general individuals and families seem to be quicker and more effective at finding the house they need. If organisations are asked to do this kind of work it often gets a much lower priority and can take months instead of weeks. Treat the project as a shared one, where people do what they are best at doing. Peter's story below provides a real example of what is possible (see Figure 27).

Peter's Story

All members of Peter's family are registered blind, but from an early age his family recognised that Peter had other difficulties. Today those difficulties would be termed as autism and severe learning difficulty.

The family often had good times together; they would laugh together and Peter used to walk for miles, and while he was not cuddly he was a 'good kid'. But Peter's relationship with human services and education started badly and got steadily worse. Peter was excluded from school after school, was put into boarding school and eventually his family were persuaded into allowing him to move into a mental handicap hospital. Peter was only 13 at the time, below the age that anyone was supposed to enter hospital, but his parents were told it was the only place he could receive an education. Six months after moving into the hospital the hospital school was closed and Peter had to attend another school while still living in hospital.

Unsurprisingly Peter's tendency to respond to his own fear and frustration with violence was exacerbated by all these changes. Within the hospital he was attacked by others and attacked them in return. Over the course of a few years his behaviour worsened as he was moved from ward to ward. By the time the hospital discharge programme got round to considering him the hospital considered him to be the second most violent patient in the hospital and he lived in the special ward for people with the most challenging behaviour.

Peter spent nearly all his day sitting in one large day room, by himself, rocking backwards and forwards. He was withdrawn, frightened and unpredictable. He had lost most of the skills he had acquired at home and now only used one word. He was prescribed with a range of drugs that had serious toxic side effects.

When it was decided to close the mental handicap hospital it was clear to those leading the closure that supporting Peter and people like Peter would be one of their most difficult challenges. Unfortunately people like Peter are often sent to large units to live with other people who have similar difficulties; these services typically cost over £120,000 per year, per person. However, the team at the hospital decided to try a different approach, and after some initial planning with Peter they selected a service provider to help him get out of hospital.

The provider began by building on the work begun by the team at the hospital. They completed an Essential Lifestyle Plan, which described Peter's likes and dislikes and began to analyse Peter's behaviour in as much detail as possible to ensure that they knew how to keep him and others safe. They also worked closely with the family, using Personal Futures Planning to develop a positive picture of what the family wanted for Peter. Using these two different tools the family and Inclusion Glasgow agreed a picture of what would be right for Peter in the future:

- It would be best if Peter lived close to his sister Kate; this meant that family visits would be easier and that Peter would be living in a quiet neighbourhood, close to the sea and the countryside, which he liked.

- In order to acquire the necessary housing a house would have to be purchased and for Peter it was agreed that the family would form a Trust for Peter that could then be used to purchase the house.

- It was also thought that Peter would benefit from living with housemates, people who could be there to share part of their lives with Peter, keeping him safe but also giving him his own space. So it was agreed that Peter would get support from both his housemates and from a small team of staff who would be selected by the provider and Peter's family just to work with him.

- Peter's funding for support was kept in a separate account managed by the provider, but overseen by the family. His Individual Service Fund (ISF) was set at £60,000 per year (although an additional level of funding was provided for the first year to enable two staff to work with Peter).

It took a year to implement this ambitious plan. While the family quickly found a suitable house the sale was not completed because the seller changed his mind at the last minute. When the family found another house the legal and banking complexities grew and grew. However, with the support of the Health Board who provided a 20% deposit, Peter's Trust was able to purchase an excellent four-bedroom house. Most of the repayment of the necessary loan was paid by the Department of Social Security.

The team who support Peter had to be carefully chosen to ensure that they had the right skills and temperament to work with Peter. In fact many of those initially selected proved unsuitable and chose to stop working with Peter. However, Peter was lucky enough to find one excellent housemate, someone who brought a wonderful attitude to his work and provided an important element of continuity in the early days.

When Peter did move into his house the early days were quite difficult, and although Peter was happy to move and the team had been thoroughly prepared for the move there were many issues that arose which had to be quickly dealt with. One of the most important problems was in the management of these arrangements. Initially the service provider had decided to support the Trust to oversee the direct management of the service. However, it became clear that while the Trust wanted to do this it was very difficult for them to provide the immediate management support required by the team. So instead a new manager was appointed to oversee the service. This change was difficult for everyone involved; however, it did lead to a far more effective service and a more responsive team who were able to make all the necessary changes to the service.

Peter's life is very different now. He is learning skills again, taking trips out and visiting his family. Peter's dad said, "The neighbours were in the other week, we had a barbecue... Peter has come on brilliantly, he is a lot more relaxed, taking an interest in things, so much happier... I've never seen him this happy, it's a hundred times better." Peter now has his own car, purchased through the Motability Scheme, and his staff drive for him. As Peter's dad said, "I used to worry about him being left in the mental handicap hospital, it is an isolated and dismal place. It was very hard to go there mentally. Now, when we visit, Peter can come and pick us up from the station in his own car."

For Peter being able to buy his house gave him several advantages that have helped transform his life. The size and attractiveness of the house helped Peter recruit live-in supporters, and its location enabled Peter a sense of freedom, easy access to the enjoyments of the seaside and countryside and plenty of opportunities to be with his family. The costs of Peter's housing arrangement, which involved a 20% deposit, are set out in the table below. One thing to note is that while the one-off costs of buying the house are considerable the advantages can make be even greater. Because Peter was able to purchase such a house he was able to get live-in supporters and so make his support more affordable.

House Purchase for Peter

Mortgage level	80%
House price	£84,000
Loan required	£67,200
Interest rate	6.24%
Interest payable per year	£3,912
DSS rate	£4,383
Difference	£470

One-off costs

20% Deposit	£16,800
Bank charges	£0
Trust set up	£250
Stamp duty	£540
Recording dues	£209
Valuation fee	£175
Solicitor's fee	£1,000
Remittance fee	£25
TOTAL	**£18,999**

It's also important to note that for Peter the use of a Trust to purchase the house worked; but it took some time to persuade the DSS that the Trust could be treated as equivalent to Peter for the purposes of their regulations. However, if the DSS had decided to treat the Trust as a separate entity to Peter this may have allowed the Trust to rent the home to Peter and to then claim funds through the Housing Benefit system. This whole area is still evolving as law and regulations change so it will continue to be important to take good advice whatever route you decide to take.

Figure 27 Peter's Story

How to stay in your family home

There is much less to be said about this final option because either you are already in your family home, or you and your family will need to use one of the three routes I've already described to get a home together. However, some things are worth saying.

First staying with your own family may not be something that most people do, but it is still an important and valuable option that should not be treated with disrespect. In fact in many cultures families gain important strength from living in close proximity, therefore if you all want to carry on living together then don't let the prejudice of others put you off.

Second there are times when living together isn't what you want. If you can all recognise this together then that is great. But sometimes, although you feel you don't want to carry on living with your parents, or they feel that it's time for you to move on, nobody says anything. People become frightened of telling the truth and upsetting people they love. But this can create significant difficulties the longer you allow these feelings to go unexpressed. There are plenty of positive opportunities for people to leave home successfully and it is better to explore those options than to live with a feeling of being trapped by someone you love. However, if you do want to live together here are some things to think about:

Adapting the home One thing to explore is whether you can adapt your home to offer the family a better way of living together. For instance, in Michael's story (see Figure 4) the family bought a new house that could be adapted to provide an independent flat for their son. Local Authorities typically have funding that can be used for this purpose and if you are a homeowner you could also borrow money with a mortgage.

Inheritance Some people may be able to inherit a house from their family, or in the case of a rented home, have a legal right to take over the tenancy.

Sometimes people with a disability are prevented from exercising their legal right to succeed to a tenancy because housing officials who don't understand much about disability assume that the disabled person won't be able to cope. It is essential that you get advice well in advance and that you and your family understand your rights and you get help to succeed to the tenancy when this becomes necessary.

In cases where it might seem problematic to transfer a property directly to an individual it is possible to set up a Trust to hold the property on their behalf. Alternatively property can be gifted to an individual in advance of the deaths of their parents. This is also a way in which death duties can minimised and this will be an increasingly significant issue for many families where property prices have risen to levels that exceed the threshold for such taxes. If any of these matters are likely to be important do not delay getting good advice on how you are going to ensure assets are protected for your sons or daughters.

Other family

Another important issue is how you involve other members of your family. They may surprise you by wanting to be much more involved than you thought. Two sisters, Jane and Barbara wanted to live together. Barbara had very significant support needs; she needed help eating through a tube and lots of help to move. They were supported to move into a better adapted home together and they had a support fund that they could use to employ an additional supporter. This arrangement worked exceptionally well, providing Jane and Barbara with the chance to live as loving sisters, but with support and in a house that enabled support to be provided.

Getting support

Often the major problem experienced by families is not that they want to live separately but that they want more support to live together, and they want more control of that support. Until recently disabled people would receive minimal support while they lived at home and would then receive a lot of professional support as soon as they left home. In fact most people living in institutions ended up there because of 'family crisis' or 'family breakdown'. But as the care system was usually too inflexible to offer people support while they were still part of a family it could be argued that these family breakdowns were partially caused by the failure to offer appropriate support early enough to families.

However, things are slowly beginning to change and support is becoming available to families at an earlier stage. The example of the Smith Family (see Figure 31) shows how when a family can get support and can manage that support then they can make a success of even the most difficult circumstances. So, if you are in a family that wants to live together then think about the support that could be available, develop a plan and try to ensure that the Local Authority understands why such support is important to maintain your family. Often it will be in the Local Authority's financial interests to ensure that you can flourish together.

If you want to achieve citizenship, if you want to belong to a community and to be seen by other people in the community to be a fellow citizen then you need to have a home. This is not to say anybody who really chooses to be without a home is wrong; perhaps they value something else, perhaps they don't want to belong. But if you do want to belong and you want other people to know you belong you must have a home. A home is the fourth key to citizenship.

Organisations that can help people with housing

Advance Housing, 1 Cygnet Court, High Street, Witney, Oxfordshire OX28 1HT, tel: 01993 709 221
website: www.advanceuk.org

Communities Scotland, 91 Haymarket Terrace, Edinburgh EH12 5HE, tel: 0131 313 0044, website: www.communitiesscotland.gov.uk

Financial Services Authority, 25 The North Colonnade, Canary Wharf, London E14 5HS, tel: 0207 066 1000, website: www.fsa.gov.uk

Golden Lane Housing, Ground Floor, West Point, 501 Chester Road, Manchester M16 9HU, tel: 0845 604 0046
website: www.glh.org.uk

Housing Options, 78a High Street, Witney, Oxfordshire OX28 6HL, tel: 0845 4561497, email: enquiries@housingoptions.org.uk, website: www.housingoptions.org.uk

The Housing Corporation – England, website: www.housingcorp.gov.uk

National Assembly for Wales, tel: 02920 825111, email: housingintranet@wales.gsi.gov.uk, website: www.housing.wales.gov.uk

National Housing Federation, 175 Gray's Inn Road, London WC1X 8UP, tel: 0207 278 6571, email: info@housing.org.uk, website: www.housing.org.uk

Northern Ireland Housing Executive, tel: 028 9024 0588, website: www.nihe.gov.uk

Ownership Options in Scotland, Unit 20, John Cotton Centre, 10 Sunnyside, Edinburgh EH7 5RA, tel: 0131 661 3400

Useful reading

Butler, V. & Fitzpatrick, J., *Home Truths - disabled people's stories and strategies for accessing home ownership*, Ownership Options in Scotland

King, N., *Ownership Options: A Guide to Home Ownership for People with Learning Disabilities,* National Housing Federation, 1996

King, N. & West, S., *Buying, Renting and Passing On Property: a guide to families in arranging housing for disabled relatives*, Housing Options, 2002

Kinsella, P., *Group Homes: an ordinary life,* Manchester: NDT, 1993

Kinsella, P., *Supported Living: a new paradigm*, Manchester: NDT, 1993

O'Brien, J., *Down Stairs That Are Never Your Own,* Lithonia, GA: Responsive Systems Associates, 1991

O'Brien, J., *More Than Just A New Address* Lithonia, GA: Responsive Systems Associates, 1991

O'Brien, J., *Supported Living: What's the Difference?* Lithonia, GA: Responsive Systems Associates, 1993

Simons, K., *My Home, My Life,* Values Into Action, 1995

KEY FIVE: SUPPORT

The fifth key to citizenship is support; in order to be a full citizen you must get help or support from other members of the community. This may not seem true at first; for we are in the habit of thinking that a need for help or support is a weakness and that what we should strive for is independence. But a totally independent person is a person who does not need other people; which also means, by extension, that other people have nothing to offer you.

Of course human beings can achieve a kind of independence; for example, hermits and survivalists can live by their own means if they can hunt, farm, build their own homes and make their own clothes. But to the extent that they achieve this kind of independence they fail to be citizens. Citizens are not independent of each other, they need each other and therefore they support each other. Not just by providing physical help, but in countless ways: from baking bread to bottling wine; from laying bricks to painting pictures; from knitting blankets to hairdressing. It is irrelevant whether we pay to receive this kind of help or whether we get the help for free. It is irrelevant whether our need for help is a basic human need or whether it is a luxury. By receiving support we become a part of a community; we create a moment of contribution, where a fellow citizen succeeds in offering something of themselves. When we receive help we become real to the other person in a way that the totally independent person will never be able to achieve, for nobody can do anything for them that they can value.

We all get support from other people, throughout our lives, but we tend not to think about it in that way. We value our independence, our freedom from others, and we ignore our everyday reliance on other people. It is in this respect that disabled people are different from other people, for it is impossible for disabled people to ignore their reliance on other people. We all need support, but disabled people require more support than other people in order to live their own lives. In fact Judith Snow, the philosopher and disability activist, states that disability is the gift of *having* to ask other people to help you. Each disabled person needs help from other people in such a way that they confront other people with that need and offer other people the opportunity to provide the support they need.

Awareness of the existence of disability, as an aspect of our humanity, gives us all the chance to confront the fact that life is impossible without reliance on other people. Life should not be an attempt to achieve independence from each other; instead we should welcome our interdependence, the fact that we each rely on each other. To accept disability in this way is to welcome the fact that human beings need one another. It is to welcome our mutual dependence on each other.

Having a disability means needing extra support from other people. This is a good thing and in itself it does nothing to weaken you as a fellow citizen. Rather the opposite; someone who needs help creates an opportunity for others to provide support to you and so recognise you as a fellow citizen.

But while this is true, many disabled people still suffer discrimination and abuse. For when you need help you are vulnerable to the quality of the help you receive. So although it is a good thing that people need help from each other, this does not guarantee that people will use this opportunity well. In helping other people we can still act in ways that are inappropriate or just plain wrong. Disabled people need help, but some ways of helping people are better than others and some ways of helping are very wrong.

Over the last two centuries disabled people have often received support that has weakened them as citizens. In particular people have suffered from being institutionalised, from being segregated from other citizens, subject to gross abuse and alienated from family and friends. People have received help, but often that help was very bad help.

In this chapter I will describe some of the things that have been learnt about what makes for good help or support. I will also go on to explain the many different ways that disabled people can get support today and offer some guidance on how to ensure that the support is as good as possible.

What is good support?

One important statement about the nature of good support was made by John O'Brien. He set out 'Five Service Accomplishments', that is five things a support service must do if it is going to be a really good service.

1 Treat people with dignity and respect

The first condition of good support is that it enhances your dignity and the respect with which others treat you. A simple way of being treated with respect is to be talked about appropriately and to be talked to directly. It is not being treated with dignity and respect when you are ignored, patronised, insulted or dismissed.

2 Help people to be present in their community

Good support helps you get to the places where you need to be, to be present in your community. Being present in your community means being able to go to the shops, to your place of work, to community leisure facilities, to polling stations or to wherever it is you need to be in order to live your life to the full. You are not present if you are segregated, excluded, put in special places or kept out of other people's way.

3 Help people to participate in community life

Good support helps you to maintain your relationships with your family and to form new friendships. In order to do this you need to be able to participate in what is going on. It is only if you are actively engaged with other people that you can be part of their lives and they can be part of your life. If you are lonely, if you have lost contact with your family and if you have no real friends then this means you are not participating, you are not involved.

4 Help people to develop

Good support helps you to grow, develop and learn new skills. learning then you are changing and other people treat you as someone who has the potential to do new things and still develop. You cannot develop if you are treated as someone who never learns and who never changes. You cannot learn if you are not given the chance to take risks or try out new things.

5 Give people choice and control

Good support helps you to have as much control over your own life as possible and to exercise choice wherever possible. If you are in control of your life then that life is your own and you can mark your own unique individuality by the choices you make. When you lose control over your own life then you are passive, a victim of other people's preferences, prejudices and desires.

So, in summary, good support is support that treats you with the most dignity and respect, helps you play an active part in your community and helps you develop your relationships with other people. Good support makes you stronger and does not take away control from you, instead it enables you to exercise choices and be in control of your own life.

Overall, good support builds and sustains our role as a citizen. Bad support weakens our citizenship. These points are really quite general and are not just restricted to the help and support required by disabled people. When we receive help from other people we do not want:

- To be treated rudely or disrespectfully.
- To have to leave our community and separate ourselves from others.
- To lose contact with our friends and family.
- To be treated as unskilled and incapable of learning.
- To have no choices and to have no control over what is happening.

In fact many of us experience these problems in other areas of life. If you have to go to hospital because of illness you may find that the help you receive there is often highly institutional. But if you can choose who you get help from and control how you are helped then you can reduce the risk of being treated in this way.

In addition it is important to note that good supporters do not have to be professionals: highly educated, fully trained, accredited and regulated. There is no evidence that the job of supporting disabled people is best carried out by well-trained professionals. In fact where people have free choice about who supports them they are likely to pick family, friends or acquaintances over professionals that they do not know. What seems to matter more than professional qualifications is (a) whether the person is a decent human being who treats people respectfully and (b) whether they are the right sort of person to get on with you.

Perhaps professional qualifications are helpful when a job is less about individuals and more about systems. So it may be best if managers, supported employment advisers or social workers operate within certain professional structures. But I think it highly unlikely that disabled people themselves will be pushing government to make it a requirement that all supporters are professionally qualified. This would be an unjustifiable intrusion and restriction on the choices open to disabled people.

How do you get support?

Now there are many different kinds of support, but overall we can distinguish four very different types of support that disabled people can use to get on with their lives.

Specialist Support Providers	Specialist support providers are services specially designed to serve disabled people. There is a wide range of these services as I will discuss below, but they share a common purpose in having been set up to offer support to disabled people and must therefore serve several different individuals.
Individual Support Services	These are support services that are developed to serve an individual. They are designed for and delivered to one individual and ideally that individual controls them.
Family & Friends	This is the support that is provided from love, by friends and family. It is support for a particular individual from the people who value that individual.
Natural Support	Natural Support is the support that occurs naturally within the community. It is not special help for disabled people but is support that is available to anyone using the relevant part of the community.

These different types of support can all be valuable but there are some obvious advantages and disadvantages to each type of support, which I have set out in the table below (see Figure 28).

I am not going to suggest that any one type of support is the best. It is probably useful to get support in a number of different ways; for this can balance out the advantages and disadvantages of each type of support.

In addition once you are aware of the problems you can also do a tremendous amount to reduce any possible disadvantages. For instance:

- There are a number of ways in which specialist support providers can tailor their services to you and offer you more control over your own service.
- There are also several ways that you can get additional support to make the job of developing your own service less onerous.

I will explore all of these issues as I go on to discuss these different types of support in more detail.

Type of support	Advantages	Disadvantages
Specialist Support Providers	You can get the chance to meet other disabled people. You have no personal responsibility for the service. The support provider may have some useful expertise. The support provider will be regulated by Social Services.	It marks you out as being different from other people. Your needs may be hard to meet when there are lots of people getting help at the same time. You will have less control over the service and who is recruited
Individual Support Services	You get the maximum possible control over your support: who, when, where and how. You can meet new people through your supporter. It is easier to change things over time. It is easier to mix paid and unpaid supports. You may have more flexibility about how your support money is spent.	People can think that your supporter is in charge of you. Your supporter can cut you off from other citizens. You are responsible for controlling and changing the service. You are likely to be accountable to Social Work and others for your actions.
Family & Friends	The people supporting you are people you love and trust. Your family will keep you connected to other family members.	It is hard to control when you get this kind of support without using guilt. It is hard to control how the people you love support you.
Natural Support	You are treated just like everybody else around. You are seen to be present for your own sake. People supporting you are expert in doing their particular job.	The support ends when your involvement ends. You may need adaptations to be made for you to join in. You may need to get people to learn about your special needs

Figure 28 Comparing different types of support

How to use specialist support providers

I will start by exploring some of your options if you want an off-the-shelf service from an existing service provider and how to go about making sure you get the best deal from any service you decide to use.

1 Identify the kind of service you want

To begin with I will try to define some of your likely options. Every locality is different and you may find that not all of these options are available in your area. I have included in this list every significant support that I could think of, even things that I personally find problematic. I have tried to describe these services as clearly and as objectively as I can; although I think it will be pretty clear that I think some of these services are much better than others at supporting you to be a full citizen.

Adult Placement Services	Some people want to live with a family even if their own family can no longer support them. So Adult Placement Services have been set up to link people into family homes and then provide the family with some ongoing additional support.
Adult Training Centres	Adult Training Centres or day centres provide a continuation of school-time support. The quality and nature of the support available varies enormously from place to place, but it is hard for these services to be very individualised when they typically have to provide support to many different people at the same time.
Community Networks	KeyRing, one particular organisation, has pioneered the development of networks of people with learning difficulties who live in their own homes but are linked together and supported by a Community Link Worker. This model is being replicated in Scotland by Neighbourhood Networks. This service is very successful at offering people their own place combined with an element of mutual support.
Domiciliary Services	Local Authorities and service providers tend to offer home help services where workers go into your home to provide limited support services. Although these services vary from locality to locality they tend to be more focused on supporting older people and doing things *for* people in their own homes.
Local Authority Hostels	In addition to Adult Training Centres the main service that Local Authorities tend to provide directly are Hostels. As their name suggests these tend to be large buildings in which many people live. Support is usually provided but the amount of support that can be offered within a Hostel tends to be limited.

Mental Handicap Hospitals	There are still a few hospitals left, although a number have been renamed Residential Campuses. Government policy since the 1970s has been to close hospitals following the discovery of serious human rights abuses and research which has consistently shown that hospitals do not offer good support to people with learning difficulties.
Registered Care Homes	This is the most common support option for people with learning difficulties and it means that your home and support are controlled by an organisation and that you will live with a number of other people who you did not choose to live with. Homes are registered and monitored by national care standards organisations but many people find such homes far from 'home-like' and the available support is normally shared in ways that often limit what you can do.
Registered Nursing Homes	These are similar to Registered Care Homes, except that nurses must give some of the support and the rules that govern their operation are slightly different. There are Registered Nursing Homes for the elderly that take in some people with learning difficulties although this would seem to have little to offer them. There are also specialist nursing homes for people with learning difficulties that take people who other services have found too challenging.
Residential Respite Services	Respite services are generally support services for families to give them a break from supporting their children or adult sons or daughters. In general these services offer people the chance to stay for a short period in a building along with a number of other disabled people. Although these services are often highly valued when people have few choices, in my experience people can do much more imaginative things for respite if they have control of the resources instead (see Figure 31).
Residential Schools	Some children and young adults end up getting support in residential schools. These have grown up because some people get excluded both from mainstream schools and from their local special schools.
Sheltered Communities or Village Communities	There are a number of organisations that have set up Village Communities within the countryside. Many of these communities were developed as a progressive alternative to mental handicap hospitals in the post-war years and they foster an ethos that is less institutional than a hospital within a country village setting.
Sheltered Workshops	A Sheltered Workshop is a working environment that is predominately for disabled people. Some people really

value these work places, although there is a tendency for workshops that cater only for people with learning difficulties to offer only the most boring or anti-social forms of work.

Social Business

Some disabled people have set up their own businesses or co-operative efforts and operate within the commercial world (sometimes with some subsidy). Some people with learning difficulties, for example Swindon People First have even entered the care business.

Supported Employment

Some organisations support people to take up ordinary jobs while helping the employer provide support on the job and back-up support. This service has proved successful even with people with very significant disabilities and is largely constrained by the poverty trap created for many people by the existing benefits system.

Supported Living Services

A few support providers will only provide support to people living in their own homes. In addition some providers of Registered Care Homes have also started to provide support to people in their own homes. Often these services are provided to people with more significant disabilities or complex behaviour because these services can be individualised and do not put people into complex group settings.

Therapists and other specialists

There are a number of specialists who offer advice, therapy or other one-off services to people with learning difficulties. They include:

- Psychiatrists and Psychologists
- Speech & Language Therapists
- Psychiatric and Community Nurses
- Art, Drama or Music Therapists
- Counsellors

It is difficult to comment on the wide range of genuine skills and expertise that are contained in this list. Many skilled people are doing good work under these titles. But while there may be some advantages in specialisation there is also a severe danger that these services, while they are branded as special, become rather isolated and are delivered to lower standards and are less accessible than the mainstream services they are intended to improve upon. The risk that this happens is increased by the fact that it is very difficult to hold any of these professionals accountable for their actions and bad practice can go unchallenged for years.

If you know what you want your support for then you can rule out many of these services from the beginning. If you want a home of your own then you can exclude services that already come bundled with housing like Registered Care Homes, Hostels and Nursing Homes. If you are looking for the chance to have varied holidays then a residential respite service is unlikely to be the solution. If you want a job then an Adult Training Centre may not be ideal. But beyond these broad generalisations the most important thing you will need to do is to find out what and who is available in the local area.

2 Find out what is available locally

There are many different ways of finding out about your local service providers:

Through your Local Authority	However, do not just ask your social worker. Also ask for a directory of local services and the list of authorised service providers; your social worker may themselves be unaware of all the options available.
Through local advocacy service	If there is a local advocacy service in your area ask them who the local service providers are. They will not only know many of the different providers, they may also be willing to tell you something about their reputations.
Ask other disabled people and their families	People who have had good or bad experiences of different services are good sources of advice and information.
Use the Yellow Pages or the Internet	Information about local services may also be available by standard methods of sharing information.

None of these methods of finding things out is perfect. If you try to find out the answers to your questions but people don't know then remember to ask them 'Who else might know...?' Even if your first contact isn't helpful you can usually find somebody who can help if you keep asking people who they think might know the answer.

3 Find out which is the best service for you

Once you have identified who the local service providers are then you need to work out whether the service offers you something that you want. To do this you need to use all the normal techniques you would use to work out whether you are likely to like the service.

Read the available literature	This is the thing that most of us would do but it is also the least reliable indicator of quality. Nevertheless any information that you get will tell you something about the values of the organisation. Try to read between the lines. Do you get the sense that the people who run the organisations are really committed to the people they serve or do they have some other agenda?

Interview people who use the service, staff and managers

The next thing to do is to try and talk to people who use the service, other families, staff who work there and the managers. They will reveal much about the organisation, especially if you don't just ask safe questions but throw in questions that will help reveal things. If you ask questions like 'What is the best thing and the worst thing about this service?' then people have to open up. If you cannot get anybody to say anything negative about the service this may be the most worrying of all signs. It could mean that people are too scared to say anything negative.

Spend time with the people using the service

The best way of finding out about a service is to spend time with people who use it. If the organisation won't let you do this then they are probably not an organisation you would want to get support from. For it would be very unusual if somebody was not willing to let you spend some time with them. If we have made a good choice, bought the right car, washing machine, house or whatever, we are usually more than happy to tell other people about it and to show people what a good thing it is. So you can expect that people who are happy with their support service will also be happy to tell you about it and have you spend some time with them. If you can do this then you are likely to get a fairly good sense of what that support service has to offer you.

4 Negotiate the best deal

Now if you have identified the service you would like to use then it is important to think about the deal that you want to strike with the service provider. I am putting aside here all questions concerned with money and I am supposing that you are either independently able to purchase your service or you are working in partnership with your Local Authority who will be purchasing the service on your behalf. So you are ready and able to buy the support service. But even then there are still some things to think about:

Purchase the service yourself

Most people who use Direct Payments use the money to employ staff themselves. However, there is nothing stopping you trying to negotiate a contract with the Local Authority and the service provider that would give you control over whether to continue using the service provider or even for you to receive the funding and then to purchase the service directly from the service provider.

Recruit staff

Depending on the nature of the support it may be possible for you to share in the process of recruiting your support staff. If you are not the employer then the employer must be able to approve the staff, but you can ask for a veto and reject any staff you do not feel are suitable. However, this will not be possible if support staff are going to be recruited to work with a wide number of people, not just you. If possible you may be able to get staff recruited just for you and have the fact that they support you written into their contracts.

Agree what will happen to under-spends

If you are involved in paying for a service then examine what happens to the money at the end of the year. It may be possible to negotiate a rebate if all your money is not spent. This gives you and everybody else an incentive to take care and use the available money wisely.

Be involved in management

You or somebody from your family may want to be involved in the management of the service. If the organisation is independent of the Local Authority it will have a management board and there may be other ways that you can get involved in how the service is run.

Get a written contract

Whatever arrangement you reach with the Local Authority and any service provider try and get something in writing, ideally a written contract, that sets out your rights and makes clear how you can change anything you don't like.

In general your power and ability to influence the details of your own service will be reduced if (a) you don't control the money (b) the service is a block service that is not individualised to you but is offered to lots of people (c) the service provider is a statutory authority and accountable to lots of other people besides you and (d) your rights are unclear and not set down in writing. For small services that you can easily walk away from these are possibly not significant issues, but if your support service is going to play a large part in your life, if you are going to depend on it to achieve what you want to achieve then you should seriously consider how you will maintain sufficient influence over the service.

How to develop your own support service

The alternative to using a specialist support service is to develop a service for yourself; this is the DIY option. This option is becoming more and more attractive and people with physical disabilities have led the way in organising their own support in this way. Often they have set up Centres for Independent Living as a support system for people who want to manage their own supporters, often called Personal Assistants. Moreover Independent Living Services are also becoming increasingly accessible to people with learning difficulties.

If you decide to take this path then you have the opportunity to think creatively about how to get support and you may have much more flexibility about how you use any available funding. Some of the questions you should begin to ask yourself are:

- What do you want your supporters to do and what are you going to do for yourself?

- What kind of role do you want your supporters to play in your life?

- Is there anybody you already know and like who could offer you some support? Would they do this for free or would they need to be paid?

- What kind of person do you want to support you? What should they be like? What personal qualities, networks, interests and skills would you like them to have?

- How are you going to find this person? How are you going to be involved in the process of checking out that this is the right person for you?

- How will your supporters know what they should be doing? How will your supporters be managed and controlled?

In the following sections I will set out some of your options and some of the things you will need to think about in order to decide what to do.

1 Decide the role you want your supporter to play

As we discussed the role that you want your supporters to play will depend upon your goals. Here are just some of the different kinds of roles that you could ask people to carry out for you:

Benefits Adviser
Some people specialise in helping people with their benefits and personal finances. Local Authorities or local voluntary organisations often employ these people and their services are usually free.

Circle of Support
This term describes a situation where a group of people come together to offer you support and advice. The Circle is normally based around a group of people who care about you and then further people might be invited to join the group.

Come-in Supporter
This describes the role of someone who is paid to provide support and who comes into your home to help you there or to help you participate in ordinary community activities. There are different ways people can support you:

- You can ask them to do tasks *for* you.

- You can ask them to do tasks *with* you.

- You can ask them to offer you guidance or support as *you* do the task.

Community Connector
Some people specialise in helping people make better use of their own community networks and in helping build better community resources for people. For example, LEAF is an organisation in Scotland that specialises in helping people improve their relationships with others.

Good Neighbour
These are people who live nearby and who can offer specific support. This can be a paid role. The Neighbourhood Networks developed by KeyRing use this kind of support in two ways (a) first by employing

Community Link workers who live locally and (b) by making it a requirement that members of the Neighbourhood Network support each other.

Job Coach

Job Coaches help people to work their way into ordinary jobs by offering on-the-job support and training in the way we discussed above (see page 65). They help you to do the job bit by bit and will do the bits of the job that are too difficult at first.

Life Sharer

A Life Sharer is a person who is recruited to share a large part of their life with you. They may or may not live with you but you would spend a lot of time together. This is a really good system of support if you don't want a lot of chopping and changing.

Support broker

Support brokers specialise in helping you organise and purchase your support. They do not do any further support than that. This service is like an independent form of care management and there are only a few such services in the UK.

Skills Trainer or Tutor

Some people specialise in helping people develop specific skills.

Support Tenants or Supportive Flatmate

Support Tenants are people who are recruited as a flatmate and who offer some support in exchange for a subsidised rent or some other forms of payment (see Figure 27). This is a really good way of picking who you live with and of getting support around the house in a less structured way than with come-in supporters. It can work really well and lead to good long-lasting friendships, but also like any flatmate arrangement you may find you don't get on with your flatmate and you need to ask them to leave. If you want to stay in control of this you need to give them a licence to live in your house, not a tenancy. For if you give them a tenancy they may have to live with you longer than would be suitable.

In order to work out how you want your support it is important to think about the role that you want supporters to play in your life. For, depending on our situation, some of these roles will work better than others. In particular it is worth thinking about whether you want your support to be based in your house like a Support Tenant or whether you want your support to be on a 'come-in' basis (see Figure 29).

You can, of course, mix come-in and live-in supporters and this can work really well. However, it is important that both kinds of supporters know what to expect of each other for you can find that either the live-in supporter feels that the come-in supporter is interfering too much in *their* life (remember it's their home too) or that the come-in supporter feels that the live-in supporter is not doing their job right. It is best to avoid these kinds of conflicts with good communication and clear rules about who does what around the house.

Live-in support is good if...	Come-in support is good if...
• You want people around when and if you need them.	• You want to live alone and don't want flatmates.
• You want to share in other people's lives.	• You like to be supported by a few different people.
• You don't want to live alone.	• You want an easy way of recruiting people.
• You want a lot of consistency in who supports you.	

Figure 29 Live-in vs. come-in support

2 Decide how much support you want

Not only do you need to think about what kind of role you want your supporters to play but you also need to think about how much support you really need. A good way to do this is to develop a timetable for an average week, think about what you would want to be doing during the week and then work out how much help you would need with the different activities.

An example of such a timetable is given below (see Figure 30). The timetable sets out the amount of paid support Janet needs at different times of the day and the kinds of things she needs help with. When Janet is not getting paid support she is getting unpaid support from her mother or father.

When you are working out how much support you need there are a number of things you need to think about:

- Don't underestimate how much you can do for yourself. In the long-run it can undermine your own development if you rely too much on other people to do things for you.

- Be sensible about whether you need other people around to keep you safe or not. Don't put yourself at risk of harm by being without necessary support; but don't end up with people hanging around doing nothing if there is no real danger of anything bad happening. I will discuss this more below (see How to guide your supporters).

- Work out what effect different levels of support will have on your benefits and entitlement to ILF (Independent Living Fund). In some situations it may pay you to err on the higher side, in other situations it may pay you to err on the more modest side. You may need help from a benefits expert or an expert in the ILF to work this out.

	Morning (8am to 1pm)	Afternoon (1pm to 6pm)	Evening (6pm to 11pm)
Monday	Get up & have breakfast Do some ironing Do some clothes washing Other housework Have lunch	Go out to work Come home & have tea	Go out to gym
Paid hours	4	5	4
Tuesday	Get up & have breakfast Do some ironing Do some clothes washing Other housework Have lunch	Go to theatre rehearsals Have tea out	Acting in the evening Out with friends after show
Paid hours	4	5	4
Wednesday	Get up & have breakfast Go out and do weekly food shopping	Go out to work Come home & have tea	Go out to Time Capsule & enjoy jacuzzi facilities
Paid hours	4	5	4
Thursday	Get up & have breakfast Go to activities at the Headway Group Have lunch with group	Some more classes and work at Headway Group Go home & do some tidying and housework Have tea	Go out to theatre Acting in the evening Out with friends after show
Paid hours	4	5	4
Friday	Get up & have breakfast Do some ironing Do some clothes washing Other housework Have lunch	Go out to work Come home & have tea	Go out to the pub with friends
Paid hours	4	5	5
Saturday	A long lie-in in bed Go into town for lunch	Go shopping for clothes Come home for tea	Dad comes and picks me up to go to his place for the evening Go out to the pub with dad
Paid hours	2	5	4
Sunday	A long lie-in in bed Get up and have brunch with dad	Go out to play rehearsals	Home for a quiet evening at home
Paid hours	2	5	0

Figure 30 Janet's timetable

3 Define the supporter's job

Recruitment is an important process, which involves taking on new legal responsibilities; therefore it will be critical to get some advice on how to be an employer. Fortunately there are sources of advice on being an employer readily available. In the following sections I will not try to replicate the more detailed advice that such advisers will provide. Instead I will outline the key elements of recruiting and managing your support and the things you can do to make sure that your support really suits you.

Once you are clear about the kind of support you want, how much support you want and when you want it, you can define the job of your supporter. In order to define the job the following documents are usually drawn up:

Job Description

The Job Description is quite simply a description of what the job involves. Usually the Job Description states:

- The title of the job.
- The main purpose of the job.
- Who the supporter would be directly accountable to (you or your representative).
- The main tasks involved in the job.

Person Specification

A Person Specification is a statement about the kind of person who would be suitable to do the job. Often these qualities can be divided between:

- Qualifications, if any are necessary.
- Previous work experience that would help the person do their job well.
- Knowledge that the individual should have, e.g. knowledge of the local community, computers, arts & crafts.
- Specific skills that are required to do the job, e.g. an ability to cook.
- Interests that it would be good for the person to have, e.g. enjoys music and dancing.
- Personality of the person suited for the work, e.g. a calm and level-headed person, a cheerful and gregarious personality.
- Personal details, e.g. an older woman, a young man.

It is also usual to separate out any qualities that are genuinely *essential* to do the job and qualities that are merely *desirable*. It is best to treat this distinction seriously and not to count something as essential unless it really is essential; otherwise you can exclude from your selection people it may have been worth considering.

Contract

Each job needs some kind of contract between you or your representative and the individual supporter. There are different kinds of contract that may be appropriate:

- *A permanent contract of employment* - This is the ordinary contract of employment which means that someone agrees to work for you for an agreed number of hours (usually defined 'per week') for an agreed amount of money.

- *A time-limited contract of employment* - This kind of contract can be given on either a full-time or part-time basis for someone who you want to work for you only for a limited period, e.g. six months. This is good to use if you know your support may be reducing in the future.

- *A zero-hours contract of employment* - This employment contract specifies no hours and is only useful if somebody is being used very flexibly from week to week. This contract can't be used just to limit somebody's employment entitlements.

- *A support tenancy agreement* - This agreement will give a licence (not a tenancy) to somebody who will live with you. In return they must provide you with certain kinds of help that must be specified in the contract.

Although none of this is so complex it cannot be done yourself it is usually best if you get some expert advice about the contract you enter into. Various model contracts are available from lawyers and from Independent Living Centres to help people who want to become employers of their own supporters.

It is important to note that if you offer accommodation as part of a live-in package that you will normally want to exclude giving someone a tenancy right as this may mean your employee could acquire the right to stay in your home much longer than would be appropriate if they prove unsuitable.

4 Find your supporters

Once you are clear about the job you have created and the kind of people you are looking for then you need to think about the best process for finding them. There are a number of alternatives for getting your message out there:

- Job advert in newspapers.

- Contact recruitment agencies and job centres.

- Asking family and friends and asking them to ask around.

- Using the Internet.
- Posting adverts in newsagents, college notice boards etc.

Once you have got your message out there you need to think about how to select from amongst the candidates who come forward. If you have done a good person specification that should help you because you can, in relation to each of the qualities ask the question: 'How will we find out if they have that quality?'. There are different ways of finding out those answers and they will vary depending upon what you are looking for:

- Having an interview, where you can ask specific questions.
- Setting people tests.
- Getting people to fill out an application form that asks them certain questions.
- Spending time with the person where you can observe them and how they operate.
- Getting references from others who have worked with the person.

If you are someone who is unable to talk then you need the people around you to think about how best to involve you in all this. In particular you may want the chance to spend some time with the person and have other people who know you well weigh up whether the candidate would be a good person for you.

5 Managing your support

Finding your supporters is not the end of the task, it is the beginning. From there on you need to manage you supporters. This is not always easy for you need to constantly ensure both that:

- Your support is right and changes to suit you and how you life is going.
- Your supporters are satisfied in their jobs.

At the end of the day your needs come first and if someone works in a way that doesn't suit you then you can ask them to leave their job. But you owe it to your supporters to try and ensure that they are okay and if possible enjoying their jobs. This means you must communicate with them and try to solve any problems that arise.

In particular it can be useful to have a clear support plan like the one set out above that describes what you want to do and how it should be done (see Figure 17). In addition I will discuss the important question of safety and risk below. One of the most important areas for potential confusion is the question of what is a significant risk and what should be done to reduce the risk of harm.

It is also important to remember that all of this discussion is subject to my initial discussion about self-determination. Some people with learning difficulties will be able to employ their own supporters, if they can understand what the responsibilities involve. Some people may be able to co-employ their supporters with an organisation or another individual. Some people will not be able to

employ or co-employ their supporters; instead they will need a representative to employ their supporters for them. This could be an individual or Trust acting for the individual. But even if you are not able to employ or co-employ your own supporters this does not mean the same principles don't apply; they do and you can still get a lot of control over your supporters if you follow the principles discussed above.

How to use Natural Support

The term Natural Support has begun to be used quite frequently; although it is not always clear what people mean when they use the term. I think that it is best to think of Natural Support as the kind of support that arises naturally from the situation you are in. Here are some examples of Natural Support:

- You are on an aeroplane and you need help, so you ask the steward or stewardess for help.

- You are at work and hit a problem, so you ask a colleague or a manager to help you.

- You are at a gym and need help, so you ask the trainer for help.

- You want to attend church but you need help to get there, so you ask the church to help you.

- You want to attend football games but you need help getting there, so you join the football supporters club.

- You want to cut your lawn, but you need to borrow a lawnmower from your neighbour.

These are all examples of how certain situations seem to contain opportunities for support naturally. Obviously it is often sensible to use this kind of support and in many situations you may find you can use this kind of Natural Support rather than use paid support. Important things to consider in order to make good use of these forms of Natural Supports are:

- You or somebody on your behalf must make sure that you do actually ask for help. The fact that help is available is not the same as ensuring it will be offered. You need to let people know that you need their help.

- You must be clear about what kind of help you need. If you need to be helped in a particular way, if you have problems communicating, if you have strong preferences or dislikes that will affect how you get on, then you need to make sure whoever is helping you is aware of these things. Natural Supports is available for everyone and so they do not involve any special knowledge of you. You or people around you will need to do the job of making sure the Natural Support is adapted for your needs.

- You must expect equal treatment. Some people may assume that because you have a disability you are too difficult for them to support or that it is somebody else's job. Politely and with a positive attitude you need to be clear that you are just like everybody else and you are entitled to expect their help.

In fact you can even do things to reinforce your Natural Support. For instance you could:

- Subsidise an employer to give you some extra support if you need it, or suggest they explore other government subsidies for supporting disabled people at work.

- Pay someone some expenses. If you want to go on a fishing holiday maybe you could pay for the holiday and get a fellow fisherman to go with you rather than pay a support worker who wasn't interested in fishing. If you want to get support to go to the football you could buy two season tickets and offer the second to a fellow supporter who will support you to go with them.

Of course the more you turn a Natural Support into a paid or subsidised support the more you are likely to change its character from a support available to everyone to a special kind of support available only to you.

Natural Support is real and is available in the community. Its only critical limitation is that the support is fixed to a particular part of community life. The steward or stewardess will help you to get on the aeroplane and enjoy your trip – but they will not help you for the whole of your holiday. The trainer at the gym may help you use the equipment there, but they will not help you at home. So use and enjoy Natural Support; by using these supports you will be seen to be a citizen just like anybody else. But you may find that Natural Support is not enough.

How to use the support of friends and family

The final kind of support that you can use is support from the people who love and care about you. Sometimes this support is also treated as Natural Support, but I will not use the term in that way. The support of friends and family is, in one sense, natural; it is natural in the same way love is natural. But support in friendship and support in family life are not provided for the same reason as Natural Support.

Unlike Natural Support this loving support of friends and family is not available to us just because we are an airline passenger, employee, gym member or member of the congregation. We are entitled to expect support in those situations because of the role we are playing in that situation. The airline steward owes the same duty to help to all his passengers. But if a friend wants to give us help then this is only because they are *our* friend, not a friend to everyone.

This difference is important because it helps explain why the support we can get from family and friends should be treated in quite a different way to the support that is a natural part of certain human situations. In fact people disagree about how the loving support of family and friends should be treated.

Some people think that the support of family and friends is natural and that paid support is unnatural and in some way bad. This is, I think, a deeply flawed kind of thinking. First if you want to control your life then surely you need to be able to control any critical support that you need to get on with your life. In practice, this means that paying for your support may be the best way of achieving control over your life.

Second if you need to rely on the support of your family and friends then you can become utterly dependent upon them, in a way that does not maintain the natural relationship of family and friendship, but in a way that distorts it both for you and those who love you. Friendship does not mean helping your friend; we enjoy the company of our friends and will help them if we have to. But helping our friends is not natural to friendship. Members of a family certainly look out for each other and certainly children get a lot of help from the adults. But the support family members give each other is part of a web of mutual exchange and contribution; the support people are willing to give must be balanced against many different obligations and each individual's need to get on with their own life.

Although my view is controversial I think that the following principles are true and worth trying to apply:

- A disabled person is entitled to a fair level of funding to pay for support from the community simply because they have a disability and for reasons of natural justice.

- No account should be taken of whether the disabled person has a lot of family and friends when considering how much funding someone is entitled to, for nobody should have to depend upon those family and friends.

- The disabled person should be free to use those financial resources flexibly to ensure that they can lead their own life, and this would include them being able to pay family or friends to provide them with help.

If these three principles are accepted then it is clearly not helpful to think of family and friends as an easy source of free support. Instead it is more helpful to think about how to use your available resources to best effect. For there are numerous ways that money can be used to get support besides employing support staff.

Buy something you can share
If you want to do something that involves the purchase of some equipment then you could reward somebody who helps you by letting them borrow or share that equipment. The Smith Family's purchase of a mobile home not only gave them a flexible and affordable form of respite but it also gave them something they could share with others (see Figure 31).

Pay someone their expenses
You could also pay someone their expenses for travel, eating, entrance fees etc. Expenses are also not taxable and so are a good way to reward someone who would have to pay taxes if they worked for you formally.

Pay for a holiday	You could pay all the costs of attending a holiday. For example, one young man has paid for the rent on a holiday cottage so that he and his brother can go fishing together. This is a fraction of the cost of a week in respite care. Another lady paid for a holiday abroad and the costs for her two sisters. This was much less expensive than paying paid supporters to go with her on holiday.
Pay for treats	You could buy people treats like getting dinner for other people after a day out. This is a nice way of thanking people for their help and letting people know you do not take them for granted.
Employ family or friends	Many disabled people much prefer to employ people they already know as family or friends to offer them support. Sometimes the regulations do not allow this and it is always complicated to employ family, but it can work very well (see Figure 31).

In my experience once disabled people and families are allowed some flexibility in the use of resources and once they believe they will not be punished for using resources flexibly then they will quickly seek imaginative ways of using those resources, getting many times more value out of the same pound as a human service organisation that will operate in a more formal way and will be unable to work as flexibly.

The Story of the Smith Family

In 1991 Jane got divorced from her first husband, Ron. Ron and Jane had three children: Robert, William and James. The marriage was always troubled and Jane had been left to cope with Robert's increasingly difficult behaviour alone. After meeting Peter Smith in 1992 and marrying him in 1994 the family were able to do more together, to go on trips together and live together in a much more pleasant atmosphere.

Two of Jane's children, Robert and William, had a rare disease called MPS III or Sanfilippo Disease. This is a genetic disease that causes progressive physical and mental deterioration and then death. Sadly William has now died of the disease, but at the time of this story both were alive and, although in the later stages of the disease, both were loving and very much loved by their family.

Unfortunately the family's experience of human services and education was far from ideal. They were excluded from several schools and offered no help from the local social work office. Eventually family members encouraged Jane to seek respite and they were offered a residential respite service that refused to take both boys at the same time as they were 'too challenging'. The only other help the family were offered was in the form of home help, but this service was never available when the family needed it. The medical services also let the family down by prescribing toxic drugs that damaged Robert's liver.

The family became increasingly desperate, living in a wholly unsuitable two-bedroom flat, with minimal useful support and inappropriate respite. Finally, at Christmas time, they came to a point of crisis. Both boys went into an NHS unit and the family told Social Services they could not cope any longer. At this point NHS and Social Services thought that they would need to put both boys in residential care if the family couldn't cope with them and they approached Inclusion Glasgow to commission individual residential services for the boys.

Fortunately Inclusion Glasgow's assumption was not that the family were unable to cope but that the family had probably not been offered the right support. Furthermore by carrying out an Essential Lifestyle Plan it became obvious to everybody that the most important thing to both Robert and William was that they were with their family.

Over the course of a year several changes were made. First the family were given the funds to employ someone from their own wider family to provide regular support to Robert and William. On that basis the boys were then able to return home from the NHS unit. Second Inclusion Glasgow brokered a deal with a bank and the Health Authority that enabled the family to purchase a five-bedroom home that was then progressively adapted to the physical needs of the boys.

The family were also given control of the funding for respite services. When they realised how expensive the respite service was they replaced it by purchasing a mobile home by the sea, which gives the family much more flexibility. Sometimes the boys stay at home while the parents have a break away, sometimes the boys go to the mobile home for a break by the sea.

The family were able to enjoy life together much more effectively after this package of housing and support was put in place. William's death a few years ago was a terrible blow, but Robert continues to astound everyone by his love of life and his refusal to give into the inevitable effects of this deadly disease. The family remains stronger and is no longer merely dependent on others. In their first Christmas in their new home they entertained 23 people for Christmas Dinner. The great strength of the Smith Family was their connected family, now this has been built on. Other family members are involved in the planning and other family members are involved in the supporting of the children.

Figure 31 The Smith Family Story

How to guide your supporters

Getting support is not enough. You must also make sure that your supporters get the ongoing guidance that they need in order to do a good job. Partially this will be sorted out if the decision-making is clear enough and I have discussed these matters in detail above.

However, it is not enough just to know who is in charge and how decisions will be made. In addition it is important that there are good policies in place describing what needs to be done in different situations. In particular there needs to be proper consideration of how to ensure that health and safety is maintained and that nobody does anything that is too risky.

So as well as recruiting your supporters you may also need to develop support policies. How detailed these will need to be will vary from individual to individual and there may even be cases where there are no particular policies that need to be written down because verbal communication is so clear and there are no significant risks in someone's life. However, for most people with significant learning difficulties I suspect that there is much to be gained by clear thinking about health and safety and little harm will be done by writing down agreed policies in a clear policy document or Support Plan.

The first thing to do is to think about all aspects of health and safety, not just the obvious things like fire safety. This means making sure you reduce the risk of any incident occurring that might lead to harm to you, your supporters or the general public. There are several kinds of harm you need to think about:

- Damage to your relationships or reputations.
- Damage to or loss of property, theft.
- Physical, sexual, emotional or financial abuse.
- Trauma and mental health problems.
- Illness and the abuse of drugs or alcohol.
- Physical harm and injury.
- Death.

The Health & Safety at Work etc Act 1974 sets out certain duties that employers and their employees must fulfil to avoid breaking the law. In summary those duties are: "It shall be the duty of every employer to ensure, so far as is reasonably practicable, the health, safety and welfare at work of all his employees." In addition the employer has similar duties to the general public and a duty to take care in spaces that do not belong to the employer.

However, certain kinds of employment situations are not covered by this act: (a) the act does not cover 'domestic' employment and (b) the act does not cover situations where an employer employs less than 5 people. This probably means that most people who employ their own staff to help them with their day-to-day lives are actually not covered by the act. However, whether or not you have a legal duty to ensure the safety of your staff, you certainly have a moral responsibility to do so.

Even if you or your representative is not an employer and you get all your support from professional service agencies it is worth thinking about health and safety and asking the agency to work with you to develop a good policy. Primarily thinking about health and safety is not about pleasing the government but is about being sensible and not putting you or others at too much risk.

It may be that there are no significant risks worth considering. However, if you can think of anything that has a reasonable likelihood of going wrong then you need some kind of plan to make sure that this thing doesn't go wrong. You can use the following process to help you think about what these risks are and what you need to do about them:

Identify risks	Be very specific about anything harmful that you think might feasibly happen. Pay special attention to any problems that have occurred before.
Imagine responses	Identify anything you could do to reduce or remove the risk of that event. At this stage it is worth quickly identifying a whole range of possible responses. Be imaginative and list anything that might help.
Evaluate options	Think through the consequences of any feasible response to check whether it does actually reduce risk and identify the best overall response to the risk. Sometimes things that sound good at first are either impractical or counterproductive. Think things all the way through: if you do this what will happen next and what will happen after that etc.
Consult	Where possible discuss the matter with all those directly involved and ensure that you listen carefully to everyone's point of view.
Act	Implement the necessary actions while explaining why you are doing this.
Document	If any issue is likely to be ongoing then it is important to document the necessary action in either the Support Plan, or in some other easily available document.
Review	It is necessary to regularly review any policies that are in place to ensure that (a) they are necessary and (b) they are effective.

Sometimes you or your supporters may already have plans and policies for how to reduce the risks that have never been written down. Sometimes you don't even know that you have got a policy, but when you think about it you find that you always do things in a certain way to reduce risk.

1 Who you should think about

It is unlikely that every risk of harm can be eliminated from our lives. For a free and independent life carries with it certain inherent risks. However, you must reduce risks whenever possible. There are three different kinds of people you must always think about when assessing risk:

- You, the person getting the support.

- Your supporters, whether they are paid or unpaid.

- Other members of the general public.

All three groups of people are important and you must take seriously risks to any of those groups.

2 Identifying and understanding risks

It is important when identifying risks to focus on those risks that are most significant. That means thinking about how likely such an event is likely to occur and how negative are the consequences of that event. In order to make sure that a risk is significant it is important to be able to give good reasons why the event might be likely and why its consequences will really be negative. Good questions to ask when identifying significant risks are:

- Has this happened before? If so how often?

- What are the real consequences of this risk?

Sometimes a risk may have been significant in a different place or at a different time, but the risks may be very different in a different context. However, if you do think the risks are different now it is important to identify real evidence that explains why these risks are different.

3 Possible responses

There may be a wide number of different responses that might be effective in reducing the risk of harm and it is important that those responses are not limited to your first thoughts. It is best to work with others to identify a range of possible responses and then to decide on the best response in the light of those options. Some of the kinds of response that might be considered may include:

- Changing something in the physical environment or getting better equipment.

- Making new choices and doing different things where the same risks do not occur.

- Getting your supporters to support you in a different way.

- Getting training for you or your supporters.

- Trying to understand the risky situation better by doing an investigation.

4 Criteria for evaluating responses

Whatever ideas you come up with to reduce risks should be reviewed against a range of factors:

- Is the idea likely to be effective? Is it going to actually work?

- Will the idea promote your dignity?

- Is the idea a good and effective use of resources?

- Does the idea succeed without increasing other kinds of harmful risks?

- Is the idea the least restricting option available?

It is often necessary to balance a number of these factors when reaching your decision about what best to do. Wherever possible this thinking should be done by more than one person.

But it is important to make sure that you do not focus on reducing the risk of harm in a way that actually increases the risk of harm. For instance, Tony was partially supported by a Residential Care Home provider (in their group home) and he was also partially supported by his mum (in her home). When in the group home he was not allowed to leave the home unattended because the staff thought he or other people might be at risk if he left the home without an escort (although there was no strong evidence of any significant risk of harm). However, it was very important to Tony that he be treated with respect and dignity and he grew frustrated by this restriction. His frustration grew so serious that he occasionally became violent and the police were called in. This led to further fear and anxiety.

What was striking about Tony's situation was that his mum had, at her own initiative, begun to let him have slowly increasing levels of freedom, more and more time out on his own with increasing levels of responsibility. All of this worked very well, was appreciated by Tony and had no serious consequences. This story demonstrates the complexity of risk. The people who had as their primary motive reducing the risk of harm actually increased the dangers for this young man. The mother who took some risks was actually making her son stronger and more capable.

5 Rights and safety

One of the most difficult problems is working out what to do when you want to do something that is potentially risky for you or others. There are several principles that are important to bear in mind when considering how to respond to such a situation:

- Everybody has a duty to ensure their own safety.

- The people who support you have a special duty, a duty of care towards you, which means they have to try and avoid anything bad happening to you.

- You have rights that mean that you can take your own decisions, even when that means taking certain risks.

- You have a responsibility not to put other people at risk.

It may not always be easy to find the right balance between these different principles. However, one thing is certainly true: if you are ever in doubt then you must talk to someone else and discuss the matter thoroughly.

In fact there is an important principle here. As a general rule good support is about helping you do what you want to do. But there are exceptions, times when a supporter should not let you do what you want to do. The first reason is that what you want to do is illegal. The second reason is that what you want the person to do is outside the bounds of their job. The third reason is that what you want them to do for you would put you, others or the supporter themselves at significant risk of harm.

This last reason is important because it reflects the fact that your supporters have two duties. First they have a duty to help you live your life as you see fit. Second the supporter has a 'duty of care', that is a duty to protect you and other people (including themselves) from harm. In extreme circumstances this means that sometimes your supporter should act in a way that is opposed to what you want them to do.

6 Checking out your plans

It is important to check out your plans with others. In particular if you are relying on funding from a Local Authority then you may have to reassure them that what you intend to do with that funding is safe and will not create undue risks. A good plan to reduce risks will:

Reflect everybody's concerns	It is important that everybody's concerns have been listened to and an attempt has been made to address any significant worries raised. It is not always possible to get everybody to agree to what you finally propose to do but you should not dismiss other people's worries until you have thought things through. Your plan should not ignore any significant risks.
Be clear and easy to understand	Any plans you make to reduce risks must be clear and simple to understand so that there is no confusion about what you want people to do. Your plan should not be too complicated or muddled.
Be clear about who is responsible for what	Often it is important make sure that you or somebody who supports you or some manager has a special responsibility to do something or report things if they happen. The plan must state clearly who is responsible for doing what. There should be no doubt about who is responsible for things.
Be reasonable	There is no easy way to decide whether a risk is significant or not, however, the plan must neither lightly dismiss real risks not must it worry about everything that might possibly go wrong. The key question is whether the assessment of risk is reasonable. The plan should be balanced as risk is inherent to all life and it is impossible to remove risks altogether. Your plan should not go to silly lengths to remove risks.
Be sensible	Your plan needs to try and come up with good practical policies; policies that will maintain your dignity, will not waste resources and are effective at reducing the risk and which do not create further problems. It is sometimes

difficult to balance these considerations, but it is important that it is clear that people have tried to find a sensible balance.

What to remember about support

I hope that all these various options and different kinds of support have not made this subject seem too complex. If you know what you want your life to be like then I think you will find it quite easy to work out how you want to be supported and I think that few of the more institutional or segregated services will seem to make any sense.

Above anything else you must try to make sure you keep control of your support and that you change it to suit you and any changes you make in your life. If you have to continually fit in with your supporters and their needs then something has gone badly wrong and you are not being supported. It is your life and your supporters have the job of helping you live it.

In order to help you remember some of the main things to bear in mind when thinking about how to get support I have written out some do's and don'ts about your support (see Figure 32).

Do	Don't
Do ask people if they would like to help you. It is hard to ask for help sometimes, but people often need your 'permission' to help.	**Don't** assume that nobody wants to help. People are often more than willing to help out and will often see helping as a pleasure not a burden.
Do identify all the people you know. An important source of support is your family, your friends and their friends.	**Don't** limit yourself to getting support from staff or 'volunteers'. The best person to help you learn a trade or develop your computer skills is someone who is an expert in the relevant field.
Do use your contacts to find supporters. There are lots of ways of advertising and recruiting staff or other supporters.	**Don't** assume that there is only one way to recruit support. Not everybody needs to be recruited by answering an advert in a newspaper.
Do think about possible shared interests and enthusiasms. If you are a big fan of the Beatles wouldn't you like to be supported by a fellow fan?	**Don't** assume 'work' must be a burden. You want people to work with you who will enjoy working with you.
Do choose your own supporters. For some people this will mean doing much more than just having an interview. Try to spend real time together.	**Don't** rely on professionals alone. Professional skills can be great but the fundamental issue is whether someone has the right personality for you.
Do think about paying for support. Can you employ staff or can someone employ the staff on your behalf?	**Don't** assume everyone has to be paid by an organisation or by a Local Authority.

Do be prepared to pay. There's nothing wrong with paying for support. There may even be people who will support you to learn to do a job, e.g. paying a carpenter to support you as an apprentice.	**Don't** assume certain types of people must be paid and others must never be paid, although clearly it's good to make sure that you have people in your life, like your parents, who are only there because of love.
Do sell your strong points. There will be people out there who would really like to work with someone just like you, e.g. a real Beatles enthusiast.	**Don't** just define yourself by your disability. If you have autism this is certainly important, but it doesn't define who you are.
Do tell the truth. Don't kid people about how difficult things might be. You only want to recruit people who will stick by you.	**Don't** use jargon or labels to describe yourself when plain speaking will work much better.
Do be clear about what exact help you seek. To support you well supporters need to know how and when you need support.	**Don't** expect one person to do everything. Just as a family needs help so does a paid supporter. The responsibility of supporting someone can lead to conflict and stress if you have nobody to talk to about things.
Do provide written information. Plans and policies should be written and agreed to by all the important people.	**Don't** leave everything vague. People need guidance and often bad support comes from not providing people with adequate information.
Do let people say 'no'. It is better to ask somebody to help and be rejected than to miss the chance of somebody good being involved.	**Don't** use guilt: It's hard to do a good job if you don't *really* want to do it.
Do make sure your support makes sense. Get support that fits well with your goals and ambitions.	**Don't** ignore your own dreams. If you want to live in your own home then it doesn't make sense to be looking for support in a registered home.
Do use your community. The community is full of resources: schools, leisure centres, shops, places of work, museums and galleries.	**Don't** rely on segregated services. Institutional services cut you off from all the community has to offer and keeps you out of touch with other people.
Do make sure your support makes you stronger. It should help you be in control, have a plan, earn money, have a home and be part of your community.	**Don't** let your support take over your life, keep you poor, homeless and isolated.

Figure 32 Do's and Don'ts in support

Receiving support is good for citizenship. It is *not* needing help that really cuts you off from people. Needing help brings people into your life and it brings you into their life. But the price of needing support is that you are vulnerable, you rely on that support and if that support is missing or is given in a bad way then you will suffer.

You can reduce your vulnerability to bad support, although not remove it, by taking more control over your support and fashioning it to suit you. If possible you should control your support financially; this is not just about controlling your support. It is also about giving a clear message to the world that you are in control, your support is support for you and the life you want to live. Support, especially support controlled by you, is the fifth key to citizenship.

Organisations that help people with support

I haven't listed the thousands of organisations that provide support, just those who are interested in helping people develop new organisations or support arrangements. Your local council or phone directory should list local support organisations.

Altrum, Rooms 10-15 Whitley House, Prestwick Airport, Prestwick, Ayrshire KA9 2QA

Federation of Local Supported Living Groups, Dam House, Astley Hall Drive, Astley, Manchester M29 7TX, tel: 01942 871157, email: indliv@federation.fsnet.co.uk

Grampian Service Brokerage, 497 Great Northern Road, Aberdeen, Aberdeenshire AB24 2EE, tel: 01224 277711

Inclusion Glasgow, Unit F14 First Floor, Festival Business Centre, 150 Brand Street, Govan, Glasgow G51 1DH, tel: 0141 427 5577

KeyRing, Impact Centre, 12-18 Hoxton Street, London N1 6NG, tel: 0207 749 9414, website: www.keyring.org

Neighbourhood Networks, Unit 10 Festival Business Centre, 150 Brand Street, Govan, Glasgow G51 1DH, tel: 0141 3140027, email: neighbourworks@aol.com

Useful reading

Dowson, S., *Moving to the Dance*, London: Values Into Action, 1991

O'Brien, J. & O'Brien, C. L., *Assistance with Integrity: The Search for Accountability and the Lives of People With Developmental Disabilities,* Lithonia, GA: Responsive Systems Associates, 1994

Reach – Standards in Supported Living, Paradigm, 2002

Schaffner, C. B. & Buswell, B.E., *Discover The Possibilities*, Colorado Springs, CO, Peak Parent Center, 1993

KEY SIX: COMMUNITY LIFE

I have now reached the sixth and final key to citizenship, which is the contribution we make to community life. So far I have dealt with keys that both make you stronger as a citizen and help other people take you seriously as a citizen. Self-determination gives you the ability to act for yourself and makes others take you seriously. Direction gives you purpose and it helps other people see your life as meaningful. Money gives you control over what you can do in your life and gives other people an incentive to act in your interest. A home gives you a secure place, and it establishes your place in the community. Receiving support both helps you and makes you real for the people who provide you with support.

But while these first five keys help set the foundation for your life they are not life itself. You could have achieved all the first five keys to citizenship and yet not really be living a full life. It is only your active contribution to the community, what I am calling a community life, which enables you to enjoy your life to the full and ensures that others will see you as a full member of the community.

How relationships develop

By this contribution you will both enrich the lives of your fellow citizens and you will also achieve something for yourself; you will grow richer in relationships. For, as I will go on to explain, the key to understanding the growth of our personal relationships is the contribution we make to community life. What I will go on to explain is based on ideas that have been developed previously by Judith Snow, John O'Brien and John McKnight (three of the leading thinkers on how community develops). If we think about the nature of our relationships with other people you can imagine a set concentric circles that we will call the Relationship Circle:

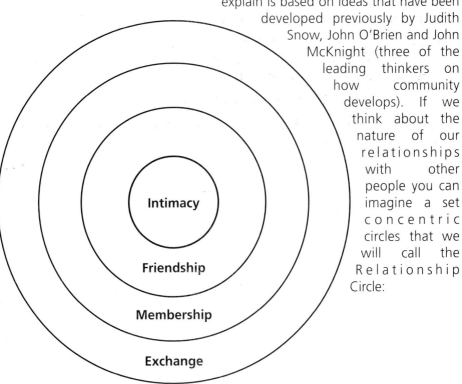

Figure 33 Relationship Circle

The Circle of Intimacy	In the innermost circle, the Circle of Intimacy, are the people who you feel are really part of you, the people that it is hard to imagine life without. Perhaps your parents, your children, a husband, a wife or lover or maybe a best friend, any of these may belong in this innermost circle.
The Circle of Friendship	In the next circle out you have the Circle of Friendship. In this circle belong all those people whose company you cherish and enjoy, your friends and the other family members you are genuinely fond of. We can perhaps imagine living without these people, but our lives would be much poorer if we did not know them.
The Circle of Membership	In the third circle we would include all those people with whom we spend time as colleagues, peers or fellow members of clubs or other parts of the community. This is the Circle of Membership, for what all these people have in common is that they all belong with you *to* something; work colleagues share membership of the same enterprise; fellow students attend the same college or school; and fellow members are enrolled in the same club.
The Circle of Exchange	In the fourth and final circle belong all those people who are in your life because they are paid to be there. Your dentist is in your life because you want to take care of your teeth. Your doctor is there for your health. The baker is there to provide you with bread. The policeman is there because society needs protection. This is the Circle of Exchange, for all these people are paid by you (or by the community as a whole) to play a vital role in sustaining your life and the life of your community.

Now this analysis of relationships is important because it helps to understand how relationships are made and how they change. To begin with we can identify three fairly clear and distinct reasons why these different people are in your life:

Biology	Part of this process is biological. We are born into a family and families give birth to new family members. So some of the people in your Circle of Intimacy will be there because of the accident of birth: your parents, your child, your grandmother and all your other blood relatives.
Need	Another part of this process arises out of necessity. We need security, health, food, good dentistry and many other things and so either individually, or as a whole community, we pay people to carry out jobs that meet those social needs. So some of the people in your Circle of Exchange will be there simply because you need them to be in your life in order for you to meet your own needs: your doctor, your dentist, your baker or your supporter.

Socialbility

Part of this process arises out of the social character of community life, the fact that many things involve more than one person. If you want to play football you need to find other people who want to play. If you want to go to school you will go with other students who want to study. If you want to be a policeman, your colleagues will be lots of other people who want to be in the police. The people who are in your Circle of Membership are there because they are fellow members of something and are in your life because you share something with them: an interest, a passion, a hobby, a vocation, some political views etc.

But while these reasons explain many of the relationships that we have, none of these reasons explains why and how we have friends, real friends, the people whose company we enjoy and whom we like to spend time with. This is important not just because friends are valuable in themselves and most of us want to have friends in our lives, it is also important because friendship is also the most typical route to romantic love in Western societies and so if we do not make new friends we may not get the opportunity to fall in love and possible make a family of our own.

In fact there is something magical or possibly chemical about love and friendship that will always defy our control. You cannot make people love you and you cannot make people be your friends. But there are conditions in which friendship and love are much more likely to arise and these are the same conditions by which community life grows and develops:

- By building on and sustaining your existing network of relationships.

- By joining in and supporting community life.

- By inviting others to share in the expression of your gifts.

These are the methods by which new and different people are brought into our lives. Each different method has its own value and each works in a slightly different way. I will now explore how you can use each of these different methods to develop your network of relationships by means of your own contribution to community life. This may sound rather worthy and a bit boring. But fortunately contribution to community is not about doing what is worthy or boring and all of the three strategies we will explore are primarily about doing things that you enjoy. For genuine communities are not built out of boredom, guilt or duty. Communities are built around pleasure, fun and enjoyment.

How to build on your existing relationships

The first and most obvious strategy for building your community life is to use the relationships you already have. Whether your family is important to you, whether you have picked up some friends, whether they are people you work, learn or play with or finally even if they are people you pay or people who are paid to be in your life. All of these people can provide a foundation for a good community life and for building further relationships.

1 Identify the people you know and like

The first step is of course to identify the people you know and like. In fact you could use the Relationships Circle to map out the different people you know. Now there is nothing to stop you approaching anybody within your circle and trying to develop and improve your relationship with that person.

You should include everybody you like, even people in the Circle of Exchange, including any paid supporters you like. But there are important things to bear in mind when it comes to treating your paid supporters as if they were friends.

A supporter is not the same as a friend

When you pay someone to be your supporter then they are not in your life as a friend. A paid supporter is paid to be there, but friends and family would be there for your sake or for the sake of the activity you are doing. Good supporters will help you live your life in the way you want to. This means that supporters will help you visit your friends and family and spend time with them and it will mean that you go places where you can meet new people who might become your friends in the future. But when they are doing their job they are not doing it as a friend.

This does not mean you cannot like your supporters, but remember that real friendship is not a one-way street. One of the most memorable experiences of my career came when training nurses in a mental handicap hospital. I made the point that people with learning difficulties in hospital often lacked real friendships. But my point was challenged; a nurse observed that many of the hospital patients did consider the staff to be their friends. So, then I asked the nurses to identify who their own friends were. Not one of the nurses included, within their own circle of friends, a hospital patient. To my mind this was evidence of the falseness of these supposed friendships. If I think you are my friend, but *you* don't count me as your friend, then surely you are not my friend, I'm kidding myself. Friendship has to be a two-way street.

Supporters can sometimes get in the way of friendship

Paid supporters may have a financial incentive to cut you off from other people; for if you became more independent of your paid supporters you would need them less. Also having supporters around you when you are mixing with fellow members of something (say, fellow students) can also weaken your chance of really getting to know the people you are mixing with. Obviously if either of these things are happening then you are not receiving good support, because good support helps you build and develop relationships. However, if you are in control of your life then you can make sure people do not cut you off from new opportunities and new relationships. The key is to simply ensure that you do not just rely on your paid supporters for your social life but seek opportunities to extend your network of relationships.

Supporters have the right to keep their own lives private

It is also important to remember that paid supporters have the right to keep their work life separate from their private life; this is called 'maintaining professional boundaries'. Personally I do not think there is any great merit to professional boundaries, and enforcing these boundaries is using a sledgehammer to crack a nut. If your supporters are allowed to say 'no', and are able to keep their private lives separate, if they want to, then they are safe from any possible abuse by you. But there is no harm in developing friendships with your supporters or spending time with their friends and family.

Supporters can become a friend

Just because you pay someone this does not mean that you can never be friends or share friends. Paid supporters may, if you stop paying them, still want to spend time with you. That means that they want to be your friend. For example, Judith supported Tom for a couple of years; during that time Judith invited Tom to spend time at her house, playing with her children and spending time with her husband. After Judith moved away she stayed in touch and even invited Tom for regular holidays at her home. There was nothing phoney about this friendship but if Tom had not spent, by mutual consent, time with Judith's family before she moved away it is unlikely that the relationship would have blossomed into friendship in the way it did.

2 Share some time together

Once you have identified the people you like in your life then you can think about how you want to share time with them. There are lots of different ways of doing this but overall these are the main ways we share time with folk we already know:

Join people in activities they enjoy

If you want to know someone better then ask about what they do, what they enjoy or even what they would like to do but aren't doing at the moment. Not only is this a great way of finding out more about someone but it gives you the chance to find out if you would like to do these things by asking if you can come along too.

For instance, if someone loves to sail and you would like to spend more time with this person and find out about sailing then just ask, 'Would you mind taking me out on a boat some time?'

This is a natural way of learning more and not only will you get the chance to try out new things but you may get the chance to meet new people in a very natural way, as you will be going along with someone who is already an established member of the relevant community, in this case the sailing club.

Invite people to join activities you enjoy

The other natural route is to invite someone to join you in doing something you enjoy doing. If you like to go to the theatre and the person you know has said they haven't been for a long time then you can easily ask, 'Would you like to come along next time I'm going?'

Invite people to social events

The third way of spending time with people you know is to invite them along to social events. There are countless of these, some more significant than others and many of them focused on food or drink:

- A cup of tea at your home.
- A drink at the pub.
- Dinner out or dinner at home.
- Sunday lunch.
- A barbecue or picnic
- A party.
- A cup of coffee in a café.

These are all established ways of bringing people together for fun, food and drinks. Some things will feel more appropriate than other things, depending on the circumstances.

These are also good chances to meet further people or chances to encourage other friends and family to meet someone. If it is appropriate remember to let the person know they can bring a friend, a spouse, a child or another family member.

3 Don't push it

One of the most important principles with friendship is to know when to stop pushing. Let things flow and don't try to make someone your friend. It never works and in the end it creates a reaction and people start backing off, frightened that you want more of them than they are ready to give. Friendship and love are freely given, not forced.

Sharon Anne's wonderful story of making new friends is based primarily on the power of building on existing relationships. Sharon Anne brought people together to be her circle. But over time her circle of friends also began to explore how they could enrich each other's lives in many different ways (see Figure 34).

Sharon Anne's Story

I first came to live in the community in 1997 when the only friends I had were Mary, Bill and Julie. I found that I was very lonely and would often phone ambulances or go to the hospital to get some attention. Kay from LEAF suggested that I start up a Circle of Friends.

At first the Circle was small but soon each member would bring a friend or a relative and soon the circle began to grow. I now have 10 friends in my circle. We meet every four weeks for a ladies night.

The Circle of Friends helped me to stop phoning ambulances when I didn't need them by giving me a certificate for my good behaviour, which said: 'Getting through each day without calling the emergency services.'

At the ladies night we talk about my hopes and dreams and the Circle tries to make my dreams come true. For example, I have always wanted to get married and so we created a pretend wedding, where I was dressed as the bride and my friends were bridesmaids. It was a great day

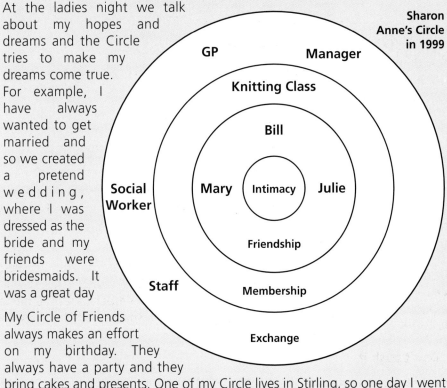

Sharon Anne's Circle in 1999

My Circle of Friends always makes an effort on my birthday. They always have a party and they bring cakes and presents. One of my Circle lives in Stirling, so one day I went to Stirling to see the castle with her.

All my Circle of Friends went with me on the Waverley Boat. This was the first time I had ever been on a boat. The boat went to Dunoon where we spent the day. The boat broke down, so we had to get a small boat back to Glasgow. I got to sit beside the captain and he told me how the boat worked. Later we all went back to Sandra's. I had a great day.

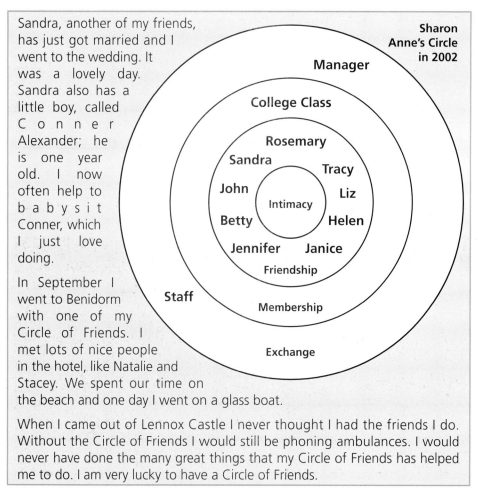

Sandra, another of my friends, has just got married and I went to the wedding. It was a lovely day. Sandra also has a little boy, called Conner Alexander; he is one year old. I now often help to babysit Conner, which I just love doing.

In September I went to Benidorm with one of my Circle of Friends. I met lots of nice people in the hotel, like Natalie and Stacey. We spent our time on the beach and one day I went on a glass boat.

When I came out of Lennox Castle I never thought I had the friends I do. Without the Circle of Friends I would still be phoning ambulances. I would never have done the many great things that my Circle of Friends has helped me to do. I am very lucky to have a Circle of Friends.

Figure 34 Sharon Anne's Story

How to join in community life

The first strategy for developing friendships depends on using the people you know and like already. This can bring new people into your life, if you encourage the people you already know to introduce you to people they know but you don't. But the most direct way of meeting new people is by following your dreams, using your goals and joining in existing community organisations.

1 Reflect on your goals

If you have used Person Centred Planning, in the way I described above, you will have a sense of what you want your life to be like and you may have well-defined goals. These goals should reflect who you are and what you really want to achieve. These goals can cover any number of areas in your life and they might be things like:

- I want a job in a flower shop.
- I want to go fishing with a friend.

- I want to do more sewing.

- I want to become an actor.

- I want to do ten-pin bowling.

Whatever your goals, dreams or hopes for the future it is important that you do not give up on them, however hard they may be to achieve. Instead you need to think about how you might try to achieve these goals. What is interesting is that, most of the time, the best way of achieving your goal will be to join in with some existing community activity.

2 Work out where your goal can be achieved

If you know what you want to do then you will also be able to work out where that goal is likely to be achieved (see Figure 35).

What you want to achieve	Places where that goal is achieved
A job in a flower shop	Florists, supermarkets, garden centres
Fishing with a friend	Fishing clubs, on fishing holidays
Sewing clothes	In a sewing circle, in a clothes factory
Being an actor	Drama classes, drama companies
Ten-pin bowling	Bowling alley, sports club

Figure 35 Where goals are achieved

Once you have identified the *kind* of place you need to find to achieve your goal you next need to find where those places are in your community. The communities in which we live are full of different places, buildings, churches, clubs, businesses, groups, centres, festivals and routines that enable us to fulfil our goals. In fact there are often many more places available than you might think. For example there are:

- Spiritual places: churches, clubs, Sunday schools.

- Leisure places: swimming pools, sports centres, sports clubs.

- Work places: employers, voluntary work places, work training places.

- Associations: clubs, knitting circles, voluntary groups, political causes.

In any geographical area there will be hundreds of such places. Of course, not all of them will be of interest to you, but if you think about your goals you will probably find some places that are the right places for you.

It is particularly important to note that most of the places that exist within the community are not obvious established organisations or buildings. There are thousands of things going on in ordinary households in every community. The challenge is to find out about them. They are not all advertised in the Yellow Pages.

One good way of finding out about what is really going on in your community is to try and identify the 'link people' in your community. These are not always the established community leaders, vicars, councillors etc. Instead they are people who are just very well connected, who know about what is going on and who everybody seems to know. Ask around; ask who the people are who know what is going on. When you have identified them go and ask them what is going on that might suit you.

3 Join in

Once you have identified the place you want to be then you need to join. The reality for any of us when joining something new is that it is difficult and potentially embarrassing. Also, as we discussed above, when you want a job there may be lots of extra things you need to do to enter the workplace. But good things to think about when you are trying to join in are:

- Go along with someone who is already known there.
- Make sure people know you are really interested in joining.
- Introduce yourself to other people appropriately.
- Help people understand how you communicate.
- Avoid going with someone who does not share the interest of the group.
- Help people understand exactly what support, if any, you will need to play a full part.

If you can become a full member of a church, a work place, a sports club, a voluntary group or whatever, then, over time, you may also get the chance to make real friendships. As you get to know people and find people you like you can apply the ideas above on how to use the people you already know.

It's particularly important that you don't go along to something new looking like you have been brought along because somebody else thought it would be good for you. If this is something you really like and enjoy find a way of communicating that to the rest of the group. They need to understand why you are there. If they think you are there because you share their interest, passion or hobby then you have something in common and people will warm to you, try and find out about you. If they think that you have nothing in common they will worry that you will spoil their community.

In the same way it can be a big disadvantage to have supporters around who obviously do not share your interest in the thing they are taking you to. Your supporters either need to be genuinely interested themselves or able to let you get involved while quietly getting out of your way. If you and your supporter are not careful the supporter can become a gooseberry, someone everybody is aware of and who spoils everybody's fun.

If you need support while you are joining in with some community activity see if you can negotiate some Natural Support. In this way your paid supporters can remove themselves for a short while. Alternatively see if you can identify possible adaptations that can be made to the community facilities to make it easier for you to join in. In North Lanarkshire the local council used money that was going to be spent on a new day centre to put equipment into all the leisure services so that people who used wheelchairs or who needed hoists could use the same facilities as everybody else.

How to make a new contribution

So far we have considered how to use your existing network of friends and how to join in community life and meet new people. But there is another strategy for enjoying community life I'd like to consider and that is making a new contribution of your own.

Usually the community will contain a rich variety of events, associations, clubs, groups and resources to enable you to find a way of achieving what you want to achieve. But sometimes you may feel you have things you want to do or talents you want to share.

A wonderful way of thinking about yourself is in terms of your gifts. Judith Snow says that everything different about you is a gift. It marks your unique human identity and can become the basis for positive community life, but only if the gift is expressed in a way that is positive.

None of us is very good at identifying our own gifts and we often need others to help us see them. But if you are someone with a learning difficulty who is not in full-time employment and has got some paid support then you are already an enormous potential asset to your community. What you need to do is to find the things you enjoy doing or are gifted at and see how you can use your talents to benefit the wider community. Here are real examples of some of the things people have achieved:

- Make and sell your own paintings.
- Organise a street party.
- Help look after neighbours' children or animals.
- Form a sewing circle.
- Offer to help with people's gardens.
- Set up a self-advocacy group.
- Help reclaim wasteland or clear local footpaths.
- Start a new organisation or business.

So as well as joining in with existing aspects of community life you can create something new and ask others to join in with you. In this way you really make your community a better place and you show the enormous positive value of disabled people.

There is one other fundamental way in which we can contribute to our community that I have not paid attention to; our ability to have children of our own. There is no doubt that many people with learning difficulties want to have children and many do. However, there is a significant problem at the moment, for many parents with learning difficulties face significant discrimination and often lose their children, who are put into care. This is despite the evidence that people are quite capable of being good parents. Tim and Wendy Booth have written extensively on this and if you or someone you care about wants to have a child then it is important that you get prepared to fight to keep the child.

How to overcome prejudice

The problems faced by people wanting to have children are typical of a range of problems still faced by people with learning difficulties on a daily basis:

- The prejudice some people feel towards disabled people.
- The physical inaccessibility of some parts of the community for some people, especially people who use wheelchairs.

I do not feel equipped to say too much on either point and as someone who does not have a significant disability I am sure my comments may be less helpful than they could be. However, I think it is worth bearing in mind a few things.

Don't accept abuse, bullying or harassment

It is really important if you do experience abuse of any kind or face any bullying or harassment that you do not accept it. If you are abused physically, emotionally, sexually or financially then what is happening is wrong. If anyone bullies you then what they are doing is wrong, you must never think that it is acceptable and you must work with your family or friends to stop it. If necessary this may mean contacting the police. VIA has written guidance on how to handle harassment.

It is important to stress how wrong this is because often people with learning difficulties are discouraged from confronting terrible things happening in their lives because they have been told to ignore discriminatory comments or negative attitudes. It is much more important that people feel proud of themselves, proud of their disability and that they do not accept that they deserve abuse. Dave Hingsberger has written about these matters very well.

Don't overstate the problem

Prejudice does exist, but it also seems to be reducing. In my experience of supporting people to return to the community from living in hospital I would say that obvious hostility and prejudice only existed in a minority of situations, although we were aided by not forcing people to live in large group situations where they would be obvious targets for prejudice. Instead we supported people to take their rightful place in their own homes in the community and most people seemed both to see that this was a good thing and welcomed people in to their community.

Work on the positive

Although there is prejudice there is also a lot of genuine goodwill (even if that goodwill is sometimes a bit patronising). Focus on the positive. If you are selling computers you don't try and sell them to the people who are frightened of computers, you sell them to the people who are already positive. In the same way you will be much more effective if you focus on forging good relationships with the people who are already quite positive. The others will catch up as they start to realise what they are missing out on and can overcome their fears and misunderstandings.

Explore how to improve access

Try to persuade people to look at improving access to their premises. If they are excluding you then they are also excluding many others; draw people's attention to the many disabled people who they could have as customers, members or visitors.

If they need further help point them to the Local Authority that should have useful resources and advice. One Local Authority enabled a whole number of young disabled adults, whose families had been lobbying for a new day centre, to use all the local community facilities instead. They put in place hoists, mats, and ramps; in this way they made a whole range of facilities accessible to many different people. This was both more cost-effective and fairer than building a new segregated day centre.

Explore legal action

As a last resort you might explore whether you might be able to take legal action under the Disability Discrimination Act (DDA). You will need to take legal advice or approach the Disability Rights Commission (DRC) if this seems like it will be effective.

Why communities matter

Of course not everything we want to do is an opportunity to contribute to community life. We all want time to ourselves, time to be alone, time to do solitary activities. In fact we probably need time on our own, in private, in order to be ready to face up to other people.

But we cannot live the life of a full and active citizen without spending time contributing to the community. Ultimately citizenship requires people to make a contribution and I have explored three different ways in which that can be done:

The rituals of community	By bringing people together, even in the simplest of ways, say over a cup of tea or by sharing a drink at the pub, you reinforce the community and celebrate the value of having other people in your life.
Membership	By joining in existing community activities and contributing your membership to them you strengthen the fabric of community. If you attend church, join a gym, attend the theatre or go sailing or do any one of the thousands of things communities have to offer then you are strengthening those parts of the community.
Creation	Communities are refreshed when people find ways of sharing their unique gifts with others by finding new ways of bringing people together.

The wonder of community is that your active contribution to it is not a negative thing. It does not make you weaker; it makes you stronger. Through community contribution you:

- Meet new people.

- Enjoy the many activities that are better done with others.

- Express your gifts.

If you achieve the sixth key to citizenship, and are someone who actively contributes to your community, then others will see you as a genuinely worthwhile human being. You will be someone who not only has the right to be treated with dignity, you will also be someone who genuinely deserves to be treated with respect.

Organisations that support people to build friendships

Circles Network, Potford's Dam Farm, Coventry Road, Cawston, Rugby, Warwickshire CV23 9JP, tel: 01788 816671, website: www.circlesnetwork.org.uk

Edinburgh Development Group, Helen Wilson, John Cotton Business Centre, 10 Sunnyside, Edinburgh EH7 5RA, tel: 0131 476 0522

Inclusion Alliance, John Cotton Business Centre, 10 Sunnyside, Edinburgh EH7 5RA

LEAF, Kay Mills, 28 Whyte Avenue, Irvine, North Ayrshire KA12 0EG, tel: 01294 271 970, email: kay.mills@lineone.net

PUSH, 46a New Road, Milnathort KY13 9XT, tel: 01577 861408, email: enquiries@pushinfo.co.uk

Useful reading

Anderson, B. & Andrews, M., *Creating Diversity*, Juneau, Alaska: Centre for Community, Inc., 1990

Beamer, S. with Brookes, M., *A to Z: Let's Keep Safe and Let's Report It*, Values Into Action, 2001

Booth, T. & Booth, W., *Parenting Under Pressure*, Open University Press, 1994

Hingsburger, D., *Real Nice But: articles that inspire, inform and infuriate*, Eastman, QC: Diverse City Press, 1999

Kennedy, J., Sanderson H. & Wilson H., – *Friendship and Community*, Manchester, North West Training and Development Team, 2002

Kretzmann, J.P. & McKnight, J.L., *Building Communities from the Inside Out: A Path Toward Finding and Mobilizing a Community's Assets.* Institute for Policy Research, 1993

Lewis, C. S., *The Four Loves*, New York, Harcort Brace, 1960

McKnight, J., *The Careless Society: Community and Its Counterfeits*, Basic Books, 1995

Pearpoint, J., *From Behind the Piano*, Toronto, Inclusion Press, 1994

Pearpoint, J., Forest, M. & Snow, J., *The Inclusion Papers - Strategies to Make Inclusion Work*, Toronto, Inclusion Press, 1992

Snow, J., *What's Really Worth Doing and How To Do It*, Toronto, Inclusion Press, 1994

CITIZENSHIP: SIX KEYS TOGETHER

This chapter is a completely new chapter written especially for the revised Second Edition of Keys to Citizenship published in 2005.

Keys to Citizenship was first published in 2003. When I wrote the book I hoped that it would help destroy the tired old stereotype that people with learning difficulties could not be citizens, that they should be 'placed' somewhere, to be 'looked after'. I knew from my own experience that this stereotype was both wrong and dangerous. I also knew that it was quite possible for everybody with learning difficulties, including people with the most profound cognitive disabilities, to live a life that was genuinely their own and to make a real contribution to the lives of others. Everybody can be a citizen.

However in writing this book I wanted to find the most effective way possible of showing how everybody could be a citizen. I did not want to make merely a theoretical argument about citizenship; I wanted to offer direct and practical advice, written as clearly as I could manage, on how to be a citizen. It was for this reason that Keys to Citizenship ended up as a handbook, addressed directly to the audience it was aimed at: people with learning difficulties themselves.

I know the book is not accessible to everybody and we are now working on an even more accessible version of Keys to Citizenship. But I thought that most people would at least have somebody in their life who could understand the book and would be able to use its ideas. Most of all I hoped then, and continue to hope now, that increasingly all books that are written about people with learning difficulties will also be books that are written for people with learning difficulties. For people with learning difficulties, together with their families and friends, should surely be the central audience of any books about people with learning difficulties. We would think it very odd if all books about men were written for women, or if all books about black people were written for white people, or if all books about the British were written for foreigners.

There is a growing market of disabled people and their families who want the best information delivered to them as directly as possible. There are 210,000 people with a severe and profound learning disability, there are 1.2 million people with mild or moderate learning disabilities in England and over 10 million people with other disabilities in the UK.

Given that each disabled person is likely to have many family members and friends involved in their lives it seems likely that disability touches most of us directly at some time. In fact disability is likely to become part of all our lives as we grow older. But still we do not see enough books, magazines and newspaper articles about disability. As a society we still seem to behave as if disability is not a part of life, but that it is some strange and marginal subject, worthy only of academic observation; as if disability only happens to other people.

I know this book has many imperfections but I hope that it will inspire others to write better books that can provide the best possible help and advice directly to people with learning difficulties. In this updated version, we have made a few minor updates to the main body of the text, included a few more useful documents and contact points and corrected any errors we found. The major change we have made is to the last chapter, this chapter, which has been wholly rewritten to bring it up to date for 2005.

The existing system

One of the reasons why there is still a tendency for books and articles to be written for and by professionals is that the whole system for supporting disabled people is still based on the idea that professionals should be in control of the lives of disabled people. This is a big claim to make, but I think if we look hard at how services are organised for disabled people we can see that it is true.

Up until the 1970s most of the money spent on people with learning difficulties was spent on keeping people within special 'hospitals'. Slowly, from the late 1960s onwards, money was increasingly spent on placing people in group homes and day centres. Today, at the beginning of the 21st Century the vast majority of funding is still spent on those three forms of 'care'. What these forms of care have in common is that the power and control over these services lies with paid professionals and that these services impose a standardised way of life on people with learning difficulties that is segregated from the rest of the community. To put it another way, what these services tell us is that disabled people do not belong, that they are not citizens and that society doesn't want them to be citizens.

What I have tried to show in the previous chapters is that there is no good reason for sticking with these kinds of support service. It makes much more sense to support people to be in control of their own lives, living in their own homes with support that helps people contribute to community life. Good support does not leave people powerless and segregated; good support enhances citizenship. But the problem of moving away from the current system is bigger than the problem of working out how to offer people better kinds of support. For the whole organisation of support, what is sometimes called the 'social care system' is also based on the assumption that disabled people don't need control over their own lives and that it is better if paid professionals are in control.

I have tried to describe the current social care system in the diagram below, which shows how power and money are presently organised (see Figure 36 opposite). This diagram shows that disabled people are at the receiving end of a chain of power and control that starts when we pay our taxes. At present our taxes go to the government (both central and local) and the community leaves to government the job of working out how to take care of disabled people. The government in turn transfers that funding to various professional bodies (Social Service Departments, providers of care, the NHS) so that they can take care of disabled people. Finally disabled people are assessed by professionals to establish what kind of professional care is appropriate; this care is then provided by other professionals who are paid for by the first group.

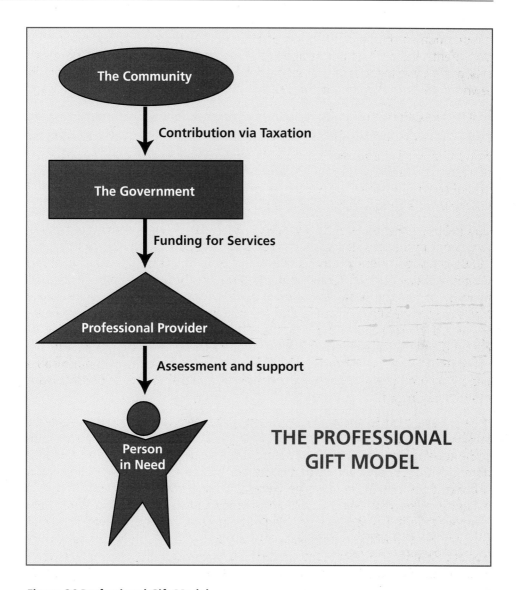

Figure 36 Professional Gift Model

At the end of this chain of power and control the disabled person is left entirely powerless, receiving the kind of help that someone else has decided is right for them. In my first book, Unlocking the Imagination, I called this way of organising social care the Professional Gift Model. For care comes as a gift, something you cannot control or reshape, something decided for you by the professionals who have decided what you need. Now gifts, like Christmas presents, are good things in their own way; but none of us would like to have vital help and support simply provided as a gift by somebody else, even if that person was talented, thoughtful and was only concerned to promote our best interests. We all need to be given the opportunity to shape our own lives.

In fact the current situation is far worse than this. The control of disabled people by professionals is not always benign; and powerlessness can combine with segregation to rob disabled people of their citizenship twice over. Even today, when there is lots of information about why institutional services work badly, these segregated services continue to be the standard service provided to disabled people. The reason for this is not that disabled people demand segregated services. Instead, like all systems, the present system tends to serve its own interests; not the interests of disabled people but the interests of the professionals who earn their living within it. The services people receive are much more likely to be based upon what is already available rather than what people really need. The kind of service that is available is exactly the kind of standardised and segregated care that is poorest at meeting people's needs and holds people back from citizenship. Changing these institutional services into better services that people can control and use to live their own lives takes time and energy and demands that the staff in those services have to make changes to their work practices and even their forms of employment. But the existing services naturally resist making such changes and so funding remains locked into old-fashioned forms of care. So, the professional's free gift turns out to be a gift that mostly suits the interests of the giver, not a carefully tailored present that suits the individual disabled person.

This may seem too strong: there is no doubt that good professionals are continually battling to offer people what they really need and to help people take up their rightful place as citizens. But the system is stacked against them, because power and control is in all the wrong places. Disabled people are not in control of their own lives.

Things don't need to be this way. There is nothing natural about organising social care around the Professional Gift Model. Instead, we can imagine a system where disabled people actually have real power and responsibility and where the relationships between the disabled person, professional groups and government are much more balanced. This model, based on the principle that disabled people are citizens, is called Self-Directed Support. The diagram below illustrates how power and control might be differently organised in a system of Self-Directed Support (see Figure 37 opposite).

This new way of organising things uses all the same parts as the old system for organising care; but now they are connected to each other in a radically different way. At the centre of this system of Self-Directed Support is the disabled person. In this model the disabled person is presumed to have all the rights and responsibilities that come with citizenship and is expected to be part of and to contribute to the wider community. However in addition it is assumed that the community also wants to make sure that the extra help disabled people need in order to be full citizens is given in a way that enhances, rather than undermines, their citizenship. So, while the community continues to pay taxes the government transfers money directly to the disabled person and allows the disabled person to organise the services they need and want. There is no reason why people who need help can't also control that help; and the best help is the kind that lets people stay in control.

It is especially important to note that power and control in the model of Self-

Directed Support is based on agreement, upon a contract, between the disabled person and the government and the disabled person and those who provide support for money. The unequal power over disabled people in the present system is not replaced by disabled people having unequal power over others; instead it is replaced by disabled people being able to have power with others as equals, through agreement, according to fair and clear rules.

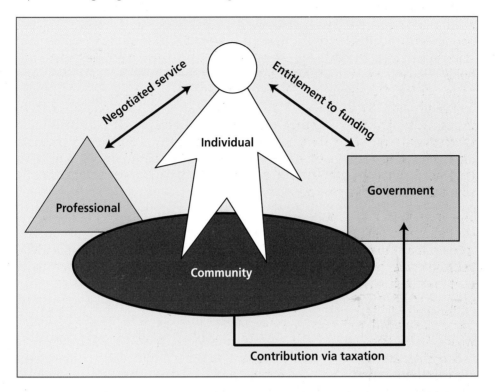

Figure 37 Self-Directed Support

Back in 2003 it was only possible to talk about these ideas as an idealistic vision of how things might be, and to note how ideas like Direct Payments and the use of the Independent Living Fund were taking us in the direction of Self-Directed Support. Now, as we come to the end of 2005, it is exciting to see that there is the beginning of a movement towards much more rapid and radical change.

In Control

I was very lucky and excited in 2003 to be asked to lead a programme that is called In Control. This national project has been funded by the government's Valuing People Support Team and the charity Mencap and it brought together three development agencies: Paradigm, Helen Sanderson Associates and the North West Training & Development Team. All of these organisations had been working in different ways to make services more person-centred and to help ensure disabled people could achieve citizenship; and all of them were frustrated by the difficulties created for disabled people by the social care system.

Several Local Authorities, led in particular by Wigan Council, had already started to express real interest in developing Self-Directed Support. So together these organisations started to develop a feasible system of Self-Directed Support, one that Local Authorities could start to implement now, without requiring any change in the the law and working within their financial limits. This system was then tested in six different Local Authorities and as it was tested, the system was changed and improved. The system was then written up and published on the internet so that anybody and everybody could use the ideas.

Today, In Control is working with many Local Authorities and with central government in order to test and develop these ideas further. Some leaders within central and local government have recognised that the present social care system does not work well and that only a radical change in the underlying principles of that system will enable disabled people to achieve citizenship.

Throughout this book I have offered advice on how to obtain the keys to citizenship. This advice has mostly been aimed at you or your allies and I have tried to encourage you to believe that much can be achieved even in the very imperfect system of social care within which we have to work. But to end this book I want to describe how a better system could work in some more detail. This will also pull together some of the threads from the earlier chapters where I have touched on matters of system and organisation.

In Control has developed a seven-step process in order to describe the way in which people should in future be able to get the support they need. This process is not yet the normal way of doing things, but it provides a powerful and reasonable way of thinking about how you can get the help you need. I have summarised these steps in the table and I will go on to describe what we mean and why we think each step is important (see Figure 38 opposite).

1. Self-Assessment

The first part of Self-Directed Support is finding out how much funding you will be entitled to receive because of your disability. The amount of money you are entitled to receive is called your Individual Budget and In Control has shown that people can be told this information and can in fact even assess for themselves how much funding they should be entitled to receive. As I described in Chapter 3, knowing how much money you are entitled to use for your support is to have a kind of entitlement, a right. This is the appropriate way for citizens to get support from one another.

At the moment people often never find out how much money is spent on their support and even more rarely get the chance to control how that funding is spent. The whole process of assessment can take months and is controlled by professionals working to rules and practices that are quite obscure. This puts the disabled person at a disadvantage from the very beginning, unable to get on with planning their own life, simply waiting for the professional to get back to them.

However In Control has discovered that it is possible for most people to be told how much they can expect, often within minutes. The complexity of the existing

Seven Steps to being In Control	
1. Self-Assessment	Find out how much money you are likely to be able to receive - what we call your *Individual Budget*.
2. Plan Support	Work out how you should use that money to meet your needs in a way that suits you best.
3. Agree the Plan	Check out your Assessment & Support Plan with the Local Authority or any other funder.
4. Manage Individual Budget.	Find the best way for you to manage your *Individual Budget*.
5. Organise Support	Organise the housing, help, equipment or other kinds of things to get your life going right.
6. Live Life	Use your support to live a full life with family and friends in your community.
7. Review and Learn	Check out that things are going okay and make changes if you need to.

Figure 38 Seven Steps to Being In Control

assessment process actually disguises how relatively simple the process could become. Care managers do know what level of funding is reasonable for a particular level of need, and by accurately describing back present practice to Local Authorities they are able to turn an implicit resource allocation process into an explicit, out in the open, process that can be shared directly with disabled people. For more information on what In Control has discovered about funding and what you might be entitled to you can look at the information on the In Control website.

2. Plan Support

Once you know how much money you are entitled to receive then you can think about the kind of help that you want to receive. At the moment it is usually assumed that a professional, usually someone called a Care Manager, will write a plan which says how you will get support. But really there is no reason why disabled people themselves cannot write their own support plan; and there are at least five different ways this can happen:

Disabled People Lots of people will be able to do their own plans, they will know what things they need help with, who they would like help from and how it will all fit together and they can make sure that getting support won't interfere with all the things they like doing.

Family or Friends Some people may want their family or friends to help them plan their support. Often these are the people who know you best and who can best be trusted to think about the kind of life you want to lead.

Support Providers   Some people may want to get help to plan from their existing support provider or from a support provider that they have good reason to trust.

Support Brokers   Some people may want to get help from an independent source, from someone who is not involved in providing support and who isn't involved in rationing resources.

Care Managers   Some people may still need to get a lot of help from the Local Authority's care managers and In Control believes that many care managers would be able to provide a much better service if they could concentrate on those who really needed them, rather than having to plan for the majority who don't.

One of the big challenges for In Control is to make sure that a new system of Self-Directed Support does not end up as complicated or as dependent upon specialists and experts as the old system. The system must be easy to use, one that all citizens can navigate around, as much as possible, with as little interference as possible. It is for this reason that In Control has also published a lot of guidance to help people do their own planning, including this very book.

3. Agree the Plan

Once you have completed your support plan you need to check whether the Social Services Department is happy with your plan. This is because you will only receive funding if it is clear that you, or someone else on your behalf, can manage that money to make your life better. There is no point in the government giving money to you and it leaving you worse off, in dire need or subject to abuse. So it is important that the Social Services Department checks your support plan. In fact In Control recommends the tests for a good support plan that are described on page 51. In summary this means that a support plan should be:

Person-centered   It must suit you and should fit your preferred lifestyle.

Clear   You should set yourself clear and meaningful outcomes to achieve.

Practical   You should know how you will achieve your outcomes.

Safe   You should make sure you and others are not put unnecessarily at risk.

Self-determined   You should be in as much control of decisions as possible.

Managed   You need clear systems of management and responsibility.

In budget   You must not spend more than the agreed income.

Of course, this is not about demanding perfection. The Social Services Department must not expect you to want to do exactly what they would want.

The judgement the Social Services Department has to make is not 'Is this exactly the support plan we would have come up with?' Instead the Social Service Department has to decide whether the proposed support plan shows that you or your representative is competent to manage the Individual Budget.

4. Manage Individual Budget

This brings us to the next stage of the process. Once the plan is agreed then the Individual Budget has to be turned into real money that has to be controlled and managed, working to the rules agreed with the Social Services Department. In order to make this happen it is critical that the ideas we discussed in the Chapter 1 on Self-determination are understood. Primarily this means getting control as close to the person as possible, but also making sure that whoever is in control of the money is competent both to act in the best interests of the person and to work to the contract with the Social Services Department. In practice In Control has identified six different ways in which an Individual Budget can be managed:

Direct Payment	This is where money goes directly to the disabled person for them to control themselves.
Direct Payment (Agent)	This is when the money goes to an Agent of the person, someone who agrees to act on the person's behalf, and they spend the money on the support the person needs.
Direct Payment (Trust Fund)	As we described above it is possible to set up a Trust that will act for the disabled person and it is therefore possible for the Social Services Department to contract directly with the trust and transfer funding into the Trust's bank account.
Brokered Fund	It is also possible for an independent broker to be paid to act on behalf of the disabled person and to control their money on their behalf.
Individual Service Fund	It is possible for service providers to receive funding for the disabled person as 'restricted funding'. This means that, apart from any agreed fees they must only use that funding on the individual.
Care Management	Finally it is possible for the Care Manager to continue to act for the person and plan and organise services for the individual just as they do now.

The key idea here is not that any radical change is needed - all of these systems of management are already used by Local Authorities. What is important is to make clear to everybody involved that there is a full range of options available to disabled people, who are entitled to decide how much direct control they want to take over managing their Individual Budget. At present, too often disabled people are faced with an unnecessarily simple choice, either put up with what we are doing now or take a fraction of the same funding and manage your own Direct Payment. This is unacceptable, in fact it should be possible for people to use more than one method of management, perhaps receiving some funding as a Direct Payment while having other parts of their Individual Budget organised differently.

5. Organise Support

Once the system for managing the Individual Budget has been organised, then it is possible to organise the support you need. How you do this will probably depend a lot on how much control you decide to take over the Individual Budget. You may well decide to purchase services from service providers and leave a lot of the details of how to organise things to them. There is nothing wrong with this and there should be no assumption that using a Direct Payment means that you have to sort out all the details yourself. You should be in control, and if you don't like the service you are getting you should change it.

However if none of the local services suit you or if you just want to get more involved in the details, or save yourself some money by doing so, then you can do a lot of things for yourself or just buy in the bits of expertise you want. In particular there are three main areas where people may look for help:

Personnel Services	Some people may want help to recruit staff, get training or staff management, or advice on contracting and disciplinary matters.
Finance Services	Some people may want help with payroll, keeping accounts and making financial reports.
Insurance	You may need to take out cover for Public and Employers Liability and may need to put aside money for emergencies and periods of higher need.

Now it is not the case that you always need professional help in all these areas and many of the details of the choices before you and how to evaluate them are found in Chapters 4 and 5. However, many of us will prefer to get help and advice from some kind of expert service. But this also raises an important side issue to think about: Who is going to pay for any support you need to organise your support?

At this stage in Control has argued that it is important that the Individual Budget should be the whole amount of money you are entitled to and that you should be able to pay for any of the management or organisational support you need. This is not the case today for most people who manage their own Direct Payment. Generally people either get no support or the support they receive is paid for by the Local Authority and the disabled person cannot pick and choose the right support provider for themselves.

In Control thinks this is wrong and that in the future most support services should be paid for by charging disabled people for their services. This is controversial and many of the existing agencies that support disabled people to manage Direct Payments are uncomfortable at having to charge disabled people for their services. But surely this is the right direction. For if all these extra services are provided for free this really means that money that could go directly to disabled people is being reduced in order to pay for these special services. What is more, this provides no incentive for disabled people to be more self-reliant and no incentive to service providers to be as efficient as possible. This does not encourage greater citizenship, instead it mirrors the existing system - disabled people cannot do things for themselves or buy the help they need - instead they must wait for services to come and rescue them. Many of these new services are far better than the old institutional services they are replacing; but surely it makes more sense to allow people the full level of funding and then encourage service providers to offer their services to disabled people.

6. Live Life

This brings us to the most important part of the whole process, leading your own life with support that makes sense to you. As I discussed in Chapter 6 you should not begin by assuming any part of community life is closed to you just because you have a disability - although you and your allies may sometimes have to work that extra bit harder to do what you want to do.

It is especially important that you can use your money in as many different ways as possible so that you get every possible benefit from your Individual Budget. You do not have to use your money to buy typical services, instead you can do things that make much more sense to you. Here are some of the different things you could think of doing to get the support you need to live your life.

Personal assistance — Get someone to support you who is just for you and who can help you at home or in the community in just the way you like.

Community support — Explore what your friends, family and neighbours can do and use your money to pay expenses or reward them in other ways.

Live-in support — Find someone to live with who you can offer you help as well.

Community inclusion — Use your money to join in community groups, pay membership fees or help you get support while you're there.

Housing — Move house or change your home so that it suits you and the people you want to live with better.

Work — Use your money to help yourself find a job and get support while you are at work.

Equipment — Get equipment to help you do what you want to do, this may be specialist equipment or it may be the tools of a trade you want to practice.

Skills — Use your money to learn new skills and improve your independence. If you don't need help in one area you may be able to spend more time doing something you really want to do.

Of course there are still lots of people who will say none of this is possible and claim that you can only use your money to pay for the older kinds of services of the past: residential care homes, respite units and day centres. But increasingly people in local and central government are realising that this makes no sense. Why should people be restricted to spending their money on the very services that people say are no longer suitable? Why can't people be creative, try different things out and find new and better ways of spending the existing money? So, persist - find out what money is spent on you and start thinking: couldn't we find a better way of using this money?

7. Review and Learn

The final step within in Control's model of Self-Directed Support is the point at which everybody steps back and reviews what has been achieved. This is important for several reasons. First, you owe it to yourself to stop and think, to check out that things are going well and to change them if you need to.

Second, you also owe it to the wider community, the community that paid it taxes, to make good use of that money. This does not mean you have to slavishly follow your original Support Plan; it would be silly to do something just because you wrote it down a few months ago when it turns out that you could make much better use of your money by doing something different. But it is still useful to compare what you did with what you planned to do, this will help you think about some of the decisions you made.

Third, its important that you review what you have learnt so that you can share it with other disabled people who could get useful ideas about what works or what doesn't work, by hearing about what you did. This is an important point because I think there is a temptation to think that Self-Directed Support just means everyone doing their own thing, what is sometimes called 'individualism'. But I do not think this can be right. If disabled people are entitled to get help from the wider community so that they can be included as citizens, then I think the wider community, and especially other disabled people, are also entitled to understand from disabled people how things are going, what is working and where there are barriers. Disabled people are partners in the process of overcoming isolation and discrimination; they are not to blame for that isolation. They have much they can teach the rest of us and each other by showing us how to overcome it.

There is another important side to this responsibility to be accountable, because of course it does not just apply to disabled people. The whole system must be accountable for the rules and decisions that it puts in place to run a system of Self-Directed Support. There must be ways in which people can challenge the decisions made by the system and, where appropriate, get redress. This means it is especially important that disabled people are present, in positions of power and influence in the whole system.

Self-Directed Support

This different way of doing things is called Self-Directed Support. In practice what it means is that disabled people can stay in control of their lives even if they need help, even if they need lots of help. What this means is that disabled people can become full citizens. In Joe's story, as told by his Mum, Caroline we can hear that excitement that comes from finding that being back in control is the start of finding all the benefits of an ordinary life, the everyday citizenship we can all take for granted until we are cut off from it (see Figure 39).

Joe's Story

Our first child, Joseph Robert Tomlinson, was born in October 1988. Like many families we started to make the huge adjustments needed with the demands that such a small person brings. Our life was ordinary until six months later when Joseph contracted meningococcal meningitis. To cut a long story short, after numerous assessments and examinations it was evident that Joseph had severe developmental delay and we entered a world we never knew existed - Service Land. And so our journey changed, we were suddenly parachuted into a very strange and scary place. In this world of Service Land lots of other people became involved in our daily lives, constantly making recommendations to do this or do that. And all the time you seemed to have to ask for permission just to live an ordinary life.

But our life was certainly not ordinary. To function as a family we needed lots of support from other people, especially when Joseph's sister Rosie and his brother Jacob were born. Joseph you see finds it really difficult to sit still, he doesn't use words to communicate and his body doesn't always do the things he wants it to, in fact many people have said he is "extremely challenging." So, as a family, we have needed help, but the help we received was what I call 'conveyor belt care.' This means that services put in help at the most crucial parts of the day based on their assessment of our needs. For example, home care was provided by the Local Authority to come into the home and assist with getting Joe bathed, dressed and eating his breakfast, and then there was more help again at tea time. At first it worked okay, but as the service increased because of Joe's support needs we needed two people to assist him. In the end it began to feel that we were being invaded every morning and every tea time by an army of home care assistants. Due to rotas, rest days and everything else, the number of different people coming through our door had gone from two to over 40 in six months. This was totally unacceptable for Joe and very intrusive for us as a family. But all the time we felt that we had to be eternally grateful for the 'gift' of professional services that didn't really work.

Not only did Joe's home care not work but he was also being sent to a school that was over an hour's drive away. Joe wasn't happy there and his connection with his community was getting weaker by the day. And it was all at a phenomenal cost to the Education Department. Joseph didn't need specialist out of borough support, he just needed people to listen to what he was trying to say in his own unique way.

So when we heard about 'In Control' we jumped at the chance of being involved. We had felt over the years that we were passive recipients of a service system that intruded our lives and confused Joe. What he really needed was a person centred approach to his support, in other words it was designed for Joe, by Joe and the people who knew him best.

He also needed to be recognised as an equal citizen, someone with rights who was entitled to his own life; but someone who was also prepared to take on some responsibilities too.

We started to help ourselves by organising a circle of friends for Joe. Basically the circle consisted of people who loved and cared about Joe and other people who were paid to be in his life. The Social Worker also came and used its meetings as a starting point for his assessment. At the circle meeting we discussed Joe's dreams and visions for the future, what his skills and gifts were, a step-by-step approach to how he was going to get there and who we needed to involve.

The social worker used the assessment to give Joe an allocation of money from Social Services and we considered a number of the other funding streams that might be available to Joe. In short we applied for funding from the Independent Living Fund and we maximised Joe's benefits. It is essential that the individual maximises their benefits, for in order to get a life you need some money to spend - a disposable income.

This first phase of money enabled Joe to employ four Personal Assistants (we need four as he requires two people at any one time to support him) who work on a rotational basis and enable Joe to access ordinary social and leisure opportunities. For instance he now attends a gym, goes on the treadmill and swims in the pool. This enables him to access an ordinary facility, meet new people, have some important exercise which helps him to sleep. We get an excellent package from the local gym, Total Fitness, for they allow any of his PAs to go with him. He visits a lot of the National Trust Parks as he is interested in history and likes to walk round the gardens. He loves fairs and fast rides so Alton Towers is a great favourite, as well as Blackpool. He also likes to ride his bike, which is a specialised tandem. His PAs need the right range of skills to support him in his varied life style and we also need the flexibility from the PAs so that if we go away for a weekend the PAs can continue to work together as a team and that they can stop over at our house to support Joe round the clock.

The management for the staff works relatively easily - I do a monthly rota, the PAs fill in time sheets and they get paid on a monthly basis. I have a local company of accountants doing the PAYE and it all works quite smoothly.

We have insurance for the PAs and have to deal with any staff management issues, which so far has worked fine for us all. Over the past few weeks we have started to break down the funding within the education system and have enabled Joe to attend the local college. We have considered how he can be in control of all of his week, so what does it look like now?

- He now goes to college four days per week which is funded by the Learning and Skills Council and he has his own PAs working with him within the college, at this moment in time they are paid by the college for this element of their work.

- To get to college no more taxis and escorts – he catches the bus like other young people, his PAs come to the house and support him from here to college. The walk to and from the bus stops assist him in having a calmer day in college. This is funded by the LEA.
- After college he goes on to the gym which is funded from his original social and leisure resource allocation from ILF and SSD.
- On his fifth day when not in college he is doing some voluntary work. This has only just started and we are trying out a few different things. This is currently being paid for (the support) by the LEA until SSD do a reassessment.
- His weekends and evenings are the same as in the first instance with the funding streams being ILF and SSD.

It sounds complicated but in the whole scheme of things it isn't and in comparison to the difficulties around the support in our lives before Joe got in control, it is so much better for the whole family. Joe has consistency with the people supporting him within his whole week, people he has chosen to be there. The support is flexible and works around what Joe needs to do, so if he has a dental appointment he just fits it into his life, just like the rest of us do. Instead of his Dad or me having to take a half day off work to travel over an hour each way to pick him up! There are also many times when Joe doesn't have paid support and we are really happy as a family to support him at this time and it is so much easier because he has been active and has had a fulfilling day.

So how will it move on in the future? We are setting up a Trust as Joe turns 18 and the Trust will manage the staff team and will have the legal responsibility for managing the finances. The Trust will be people who love and care about Joe, and it will be developed so it is sustainable, as we, his parents, get older. After all I never wanted to be his care manager, his accountant or his director of services, all I ever wanted to be is just Joe's Mum - bring on the washing!

Figure 39 Joe's Story

Finally I want to return to a philosophical point. Citizenship is not important because we are all the same. We are not all the same; each of us varies in many ways one from another and disabled people are just one particular group of people who vary from the norm because of the disadvantages they face in life. But whether you celebrate the great advantages that flow from human diversity, or whether you would prefer that there was more uniformity between human beings, it is a fact that diversity keeps creeping in.

Citizenship matters because we are different. The very fact that we are different makes us vulnerable to prejudice, exclusion and segregation, as the history of disability shows. But a commitment to citizenship gives us the chance to fight the human tendency to exploit the disadvantages of others. This will never be simply a matter of changing a law or of reorganising services. We will need to be constantly alert to the possibility that others are being cut out of community.

For In Control we have tried to distil down the key principles that we think experience shows act to support disabled people in their citizenship. These principles may not be eternally relevant, but they seem to us to capture the key challenges we face today in ensuring that all disabled people are enabled to be full citizens:

1. Right to Independent Living

If someone has an impairment which means they need help to fulfil their role as a citizen, then they should get the help they need.I can get the support I need to be an independent citizen.

2. Right to an Individual Budget

If someone needs ongoing paid help as part of their life then they should be able to decide how the money that pays for that help should be used.I know how much money I can use for my support.

3. Right to Self-Determination

If someone needs help to make decisions, then decision-making should be made as close to the person as possible, reflecting the person's own interests and preferences.I have the authority, support or representation to make my own decisions.

4. Right to Accessibility

The system of rules within which people have to work must be clear and open to maximise the ability of the disabled person to take control of their own support. I can understand the rules and systems and am able to get help easily.

5. Right to Flexible Funding

When someone is using their Individual Budget they should be free to spend their funds in the way that makes best sense to them, without unnecessary restrictions.I can use my money flexibly and creatively.

6. Accountability Principle

The disabled person and the government both have a responsibility to each other to explain their decisions and to share what they have learnt. I should tell people how I used my money and anything I've learnt.

7. Capacity Principle

Disabled people, their families and their communities must not be assumed to be incapable of managing their own support, learning skills and making a contribution.Give me enough help, but not too much; I've got something to contribute too.I hope you have found this book useful and I hope that in the future your story, the story of what you achieved with your life, can be shared by your friends in your community. And if you want to share it with others please submit it to In Control. Perhaps we could also include it in the next edition of Keys to Citizenship.